Also by Danielle Kartes

Rustic Joyful Food: My Heart's Table
Rustic Joyful Food: Generations
Rustic Joyful Food: Meant to Share

You Were Always There

My Very First Cookbook
Mom and Me Cooking Together
Dad and Me Fun in the Kitchen
Grandma and Me in the Kitchen
Grandpa and Me Learn to Cook
A Recipe for How Much I Miss You
A Recipe for How Much I Love You

BUTTER, FLOUR, SUGAR,
joy

DANIELLE KARTES

Photography by Michael Kartes

 sourcebooks

Published by Sourcebooks
P.O. Box 4410, Naperville, Illinois 60567-4410
(630) 961-3900
sourcebooks.com

Cataloging-in-Publication Data is on file with the Library of Congress.

Printed and bound in China.
OGP 10 9 8 7 6 5 4 3 2 1

FOR MIKE, NOAH, AND MILO

The cake to my icing, the joy to my heart

Contents

Bars and Bakes 67

Pies and Galettes 113

Introduction

A WILD WELCOME

This book flies in the face of all other baking books. Here you'll find shortcuts, deleted steps, and simplified everything. No more adding in thirds to get the perfect crumb; instead, dump-and-stir techniques reign supreme in this book. And getting here wasn't easy.

When I first started baking, I wanted every shortcut, but I wasn't naturally a good baker. Get a scale, they said! Measure and spoon and level, they said! Check the internal temperature for doneness with a thermometer (208 degrees Fahrenheit is the magic number for cake, in case you are wondering). Use only the best ingredients! Were they wrong? No, everything you've heard about baking is true. It's chemistry.

But how does a whimsical girl who loves to cook and measure with her heart write a baking book for people who don't bake? I mean, I wanted to write this book years ago. I thought it'd be simple. I thought I'd use the knowledge I had at the time, and magically I'd come up with something fabulous for home cooks everywhere. But I had to go back to the drawing board. I am not in the habit of using someone else's recipe for reference, then crafting my own version of their creation. I'll take a basic cake recipe I've used for years, for instance, one maybe that started with my mom, and then modify or add to *that* to make a new version. This method will get you by, but it won't produce brilliance every time. I learned the hard way that to rewrite the rules I needed a full-blown, two-year crash-course education in baking. I kicked against the goads for a little bit but eventually got to work.

I began to learn; it was trial by fire. This ailed my bend-the-rules heart, but after I settled into a routine (dirtying *every* bowl, reading up on how the French bake, and teaching myself to appreciate each painstaking process necessary to achieve the perfect cake), I was able to start the true work. I made a million cakes that failed. I tried a billion cookie shortcuts that failed. I tried desperately to measure with my heart and failed. But during all the failing, I picked up little things along the way, these little tips. Like, who wants to dirty fourteen mixing bowls making a cake? Not me, so I just mix all the cake's wet ingredients in a bowl, then put a metal sieve over the bowl and dump in the dry ingredients. This tip eliminates extra dishes, manifests calmness (because, hey, less mess!), and sifts the flour so it's light and lump-free hitting the batter.

When I first began cooking and baking, I desperately wanted to be like my mother and her grandmother before her. In our little kitchen, my mom

> "There is something to be said for the simplicity of making a cake in the middle of the week. No fancy house, oven, or ingredients necessary."

would make chocolate chip cookies and just dump things in, no measuring cup in sight, then mix by hand and dump in a little more. She knew exactly what to look for. Her cookies were perfect: chewy and delightful. I'd try to do the same thing in my first apartment. I thought, *Okay, here we go! I've got a home of my own and I'm a baker now. Just dump and stir!*

Hockey pucks! Why didn't my stuff work? I hated using recipes, but honestly, I needed practice. I needed to allow myself to learn what made a good cookie. There was a lot of living I couldn't see that went into my mother's great chocolate chip cookies. You don't just start out good at something, but with enough practice, experience, and living, you will end up good at that something.

It's taken me years to collect these recipes, years of failing into ultimate success and years of authentic living to collect a pile of simple, reliable, foolproof sweets like the Bank Ladies Upside-Down German Chocolate Cake or Coconut Macaroons. The choose-your-own-adventure pie fillings are a favorite of mine because it's one method along with endless combos of fruits. Every cake, cookie, and pie in this book has a story. I've managed to simplify each one and come up with incredible results—results worthy of a book about simple sweets, one-bowl wonders with the least number of steps and the best possible outcome.

There is something to be said for the simplicity of making a cake in the middle of the week. No fancy house, oven, or ingredients necessary. All you need is to stock up on butter, flour, sugar, and joy! Yes, joy, the most important ingredient in *anything* you make. And pie! Pie hits the reset button like nothing else does. Dessert is a small break in time; just a touch of sugar before bed—no matter what the experts say—is a good thing. I'm not talking about overindulgence but about living life to the fullest. Sweets are pure, unfiltered vehicles for joy. There is something so happy about dessert! And you will become a better baker with these recipes, I promise.

Life comes at you fast. With two small boys and the pressures of running a business among many—*so many*—other things, I spent a recent summer feeling the wisp of burnout. Trying to get all of the things done and be a good mom and a good wife and make sure I was still providing for my family alongside my husband had me feeling overwhelmed and exhausted. Sometimes we wake up and go about our day oblivious to the reality that we've been swallowed up by the to-do list. It just happens; we begin connecting the dots, waking up tired, then daydreaming of going back to bed by 10:00 a.m.

In the midst of this special time with small children in the home, exhaustion presents itself alongside the highs of motherhood. The good stuff is *really* good: small hands clutching cake you've just made; piles of endless crumbs in, on, and around everything; sweet and precious smiles and tiny teeth—and a flood of emotions about just how beautiful and delightful our children are. There are days we've barely managed to brush our own teeth, but we *have to* head back to school to drop off that morning's for-gotten brown-bag lunch with an extra cookie, and it's recess time, so we opt to walk the lunch down to the playground for that great big hug. I sort of *live* for these moments. This time, while my kids are small, is short and precious, and I love it more than I have any other time in my life. My oldest son, Noah, is slowly losing all those baby-boy things I thought for

"You don't just start out good at something, but with enough practice, experience, and living, you will end up good at that something."

"Like anyone, I have regrets some days, but then, thankfully, I'm blessed with a bit of perspective. Without my total mess-ups I wouldn't have learned what not to do the next go-round. I wouldn't have learned. That's key."

sure would last forever. Thank God that in the midst of the growing he still snuggles his mama. He loves one-on-one time and to tell me of all of the newest things he's discovered on his tablet. Some days, I think about his baby teeth and I cry.

One thing my husband and I have always maintained in this growing process is an intentionality in enjoying every phase of our boys growing up. I've grown up right alongside these children. We work to never miss out on the wonder and joy of observing this growth, even while we desperately want sleep or to stop bargaining at the dinner table in the face of tearful protests over that uneaten plate of food. We've loved, and continue to love, every bit of raising these children. One day they will be men. We will not have done it perfectly, but we will have done it with perfectly wild love.

Like anyone, I have regrets some days, but then, thankfully, I'm blessed with a bit of perspective. Without my total mess-ups I wouldn't have learned what not to do the next go-round. I wouldn't have learned. That's key. I was talking with my husband recently about childhood, and I said, "Gosh, I miss being a kid!" Then, I quickly took it back. I love things about my childhood, but I love my life now so fiercely, even in the burnout, that I'd never long to turn back time. Sure, I look at pictures of my children and terribly miss the smaller versions of them; it is an ache I'll never be able to shake. But I adore the current phase I'm in, always. Time, I realize, is not a thief—it is my ally. Life will move in and out and ebb and flow, but if I'm able to slow down and enjoy the moment *in the moment*, time will always be on my side.

Where we live, there are many stunning farms nearby and a river that runs through the area, peeking in and out as we round bends on afternoon drives. When life feels out of control, I like to pile into the car with the boys and drive into the countryside. Some days we get french fries from the burger shack in Fall City, and some days we just drive. On one particular afternoon in August, I noticed a field of dahlias. I had never noticed this field full of flowers before, although we had driven past it many times. I made Mike turn in. This was a private farm, not a you-cut operation open to the public. There were no buildings nearby, just a handful of cars in a small dirt lot, a few people working in the rows. One woman was walking to her car. We pulled up, and I rolled my window down. "Hello," I called out to her. "Can I help you?" she asked, smiling. I said, "Yes, I can't help but notice this amazing field. I'm having family pictures next week. Would I be able to come here?" She said, "Sure! My sister should be here. Just let her know you spoke with me. That should be fine."

The day to take photos arrived, and it had been a hard day, emotional, the kind of day that is never-ending and full of tasks. The kind of day where your children don't listen and your spouse speaks sharply. Work had been butting up against the pressures of providing a fun summer for the kids, leaving little in the way of time for running our little business. Nevertheless, we piled into the car and set out for the dahlia farm. The sister of the woman we had met before graciously ushered us into the fields, letting us know her parents were out there working and they'd be happy to answer any questions we might have. The evening light was lovely and the fields were breathtaking, but when I got out of the car, I was tense. I could feel a lump in the back of my throat.

Our photographer met us, and we began taking pictures. We hid our struggles of the day behind smiles and laughs. It was hot, and my youngest son, Milo, had no designs on keeping things running smoothly. But we did our best, holding hands, roaming the fields, and posing in the rows. Dahlias, if you've not breathed in their fragrance, have a beautiful, green smell. The scent differs from a sweet-smelling flower like a lilac or rose. They give off no perfume; rather, it is a comforting, almost vegetal, smell. I love the scent of dahlias. They towered over me. The flower heads crisscrossed and bent above my head as if to provide a bit of protection from the things I was feeling. I saw no one working. It was a colorful little universe, just us and these breathtaking flowers, acres and acres of peace and beauty.

At one point, a small man emerged from one of the rows. He was all of five feet tall, in his late seventies. A basket was hoisted onto his back, a bunch of cut white dahlias as tall as he was springing out on all sides. We made eye contact as my children tromped and hollered and laughed ahead of me. I opened my mouth to explain why we were in his lovely field, but before the words came, he softly said, "Enjoy!" His smile was big and earnest, his body language open. It was a simple direction: enjoy. I was stunned. I profusely thanked him and made mention of how beautiful everything was, but he paid no mind, just nodded and smiled and shifted the massive flowers on his back. Just as quickly as he appeared, he was on his way.

This man had never met me before, had no idea who I was or why I was there in his fields. And he didn't care. He just invited me to enjoy his hard work. Isn't this like how our Heavenly Father provides for us? How splendid to drink in the beauty of where I was and to be inside that moment. We finished our photos. I felt that there had been some kind of breakthrough. It was time to leave, and I found myself not wanting to go. Michael got the kids in the car.

I slowly walked through a row to take in all the flowers one last time. I trudged through the sandy, dusty soil and saw my new friend emerge from another row with freshly cut bundles. I nodded to him and smiled. If someone had come to my home to wander around, would I have been so gracious? Would I have invited the stranger in? I don't think I would have.

As we drove away I couldn't stop thinking about the entire experience. We saw a massive elk standing stone-still in a pasture off the side of the road and pulled over to revel in its beauty. It felt like a sign. I'd never seen an elk so big. I'd also never experienced grace so big. I couldn't help but think that God used that man and the elk to invite me back to enjoying life again, to remind me to drink in the moments, to help me understand that I'm here for one purpose: to live wildly and enjoy this life. Happiness is in my makeup. I am a glass-half-full girl. I am the one who always strives to look on the bright side. I don't want to take life too seriously, but every so often I get taken in by the pressures, and when I'm gasping for air, I realize what I've done and try to pick up the pieces while holding back tears. The dahlias are blooming here now as I write this, and they fill my eyes with happy tears. These big, pretty flowers ask me each time I see them to slow down and remember why I'm here. My babies are bigger and life is still complicated, but it's a damn good time. I will never forget the day a stranger invited me to enjoy the works of his hands with no questions asked. God has this perfect plan, you know? I just need to settle in for it.

It's easy to sometimes forget to enjoy life. Isn't that so true? So busy living that we forget to live. It's one thing to be alive, but another thing entirely to truly live. I invite you to slow down, breathe deep, and take in the wonder that is this life, with all its flaws and misgivings. I invite you, when things are tough, to direct your attention to the sweeter side of life. It is in that spirit that I present these recipes to you. Having said that, kiss your loved ones, get them into the kitchen with you, and mix up a big batch of the best Ultimate Rye Chocolate Chip Cookies you've ever tasted. Or pick a cake, pie, or pudding! Oh, the pudding section is a dream! The panna cotta with passion fruit and the Swedish cream with port wine and fresh berries: these bits and bobbles are truly the joie de vivre, the joy of life.

And remember that all this truly is, in spite of its challenges and trials, a life full of butter, flour, sugar, and joy.

I'm glad you are here. Let's make something sweet.

> "And remember that all this truly is, in spite of its challenges and trials, a life full of butter, flour, sugar, and joy."

Food for a
Baker's Thoughts

When I set out to test a swath of recipes with my recipe tester Susan, she asked me some questions I found very valuable. She wanted to get a sense of what kind of baker I was, and answering them gave me a clearer picture of my style in the kitchen. I thought you might like to ask yourself this set of questions as well, to help you define your own baking style.

◆ **Are you a "scoop from the flour container, then level off" baker OR a "spoon the flour into a measuring cup, then level off" baker?**
I am a through-and-through "scoop from the bag" kind of girl. This means, for instance, my 1¾ cup of flour scooped from the bag equals roughly 2 cups measured by the spoon-and-level baker.

◆ **Is there a particular brand of flour that you would like me to test with? King Arthur, Gold Medal, etc.**
I tested multiple brands of flour for each recipe. It was very important to me to really dig deep and make sure that these recipes worked with the major brands offered at the grocery store. Choose your favorite!

◆ **Do you always use large eggs?**
Large and XL, baby! Purchase whichever is on sale, but I'll get the big guys if they are in my price range. If I find that my eggs are on the smaller side, I add another.

◆ **Do you always use unsalted butter?**
Always salted; I like salted butter and more salt in each recipe. It makes a big difference in the result being more flavorful.

◆ **When you use milk, sour cream, eggs, etc., for baking (like in a batter), do you let them sit at room temperature or straight from the refrigerator?**
I do both, and I tested both for this book. Some days, I have an hour to allow items to come to room temperature, and some days, the eggs will be lingering on the counter from breakfast and the butter and milk come straight from the fridge.

Here are some bits of information I found helpful when creating this book:

- A metal pan bakes a better cake.
- A metal mesh sieve saves the day over and over again. You can do this instead of sifting anything every time.
- Butter can be melted for 10 to 15 seconds in the microwave.
- For all my gluten-free peeps, simply swap your favorite gluten-free flour 1:1 for any recipe that calls for all-purpose flour.

What is Dutch process cocoa powder?

Dutch process means that the cocoa is washed or treated with an alkaline agent to give the chocolate a smoother, less acidic bite. For me, it's less fruity, as sometimes chocolate can have a lovely, fruity note. Never fear, you'll absolutely never need to buy a specialty Dutch process cocoa powder for my recipes. All unsweetened cocoa powder is interchangeable. Some brands have more starch, resulting in a slightly different bake, but none of these recipes presents a notable difference. We are not pastry chefs; we are home cooks. Your cocoa powder choice is a free one!

What is cake flour?

Cake flour is simply flour and cornstarch mixed. I always take 1 cup of flour, remove one tablespoon, and add one tablespoon of cornstarch, then whisk well. Voila! Your very own cake flour. The cornstarch adds that lightness that's so desirable in cake.

What is castor sugar?

It's white granulated sugar that's a bit finer than standard white granulated sugar. It's also advertised as "super-fine" white sugar.

What is muscovado?

Muscovado is unrefined brown sugar. It even has trace minerals and antioxidants because it hasn't gone through the refining process. It retains all its molasses, none removed. It's very rich in color and has a lovely dark toffee flavor.

What is the difference between dark and light brown sugar?

Each simply represents a different step in the refining process.

Are all salts created equal?

Nope. In recipes I always call for kosher salt, which has a larger crystal and softer taste, and flaky sea salt for finishing. If table salt is all you have, I generally use half the called-for amount.

Happy Baking!

Cookies

A DELIGHTFUL SETUP FOR BETTER BAKING

What is it about a cookie that just makes us smile?

I like to think of cookies as the gateway to good baking. I think if you can make a great cookie, you can make anything sweet. If you can manage to turn your cookies from hockey pucks into tender, delightful, melt-in-your-mouth treats, you've really won. These portable, chewy, crispy, and buttery disks of pure love simply create *happiness*.

When I first set out on my baking journey some twenty-five years ago, I wanted so badly to be the lady who effortlessly dumps ingredients into a bowl and—*voila!*—pulls a bakery-worthy treat from the oven, no effort at all. Truth be told, my cookies were terrible: tough, floury, and not at all the cookies I'd dreamt of making. But I refused to look at recipes! I thought I could wing it.

But as age got ahold of me, along with a bit of common sense, I began to see the light. I started to read recipes and make better cookies...but they still weren't great. Honestly, I was a little scared of recipes. I'd follow them *perfectly* to eliminate room for error, but I would forget the one key component to any solid baked good of quality: me. I was leaving out my intuition and my ideas. I was leaving *me* out of the process.

When I set out to write this book, I had an idea of what I wanted it to be and how I wanted it to read. But it wasn't working. Turns out I needed a wild education in baking. To demystify and change the rules, I had to learn the rules and reasons for why we do what we do when we bake; I had to educate myself on the science bits behind every rule. As I write this, the deadline for submitting this book to the publisher came a year ago. But if I'd turned it in a year ago, the magical things I learned throughout this year—things like using my innate cook's sense to bake beautifully—wouldn't have come to pass. All this is to say that good things take time. Great bakers aren't made overnight. I know I wasn't. I also stopped telling myself I wasn't a good baker. I am a fabulous baker! I'm just a baker who lacks patience despite my desire for perfection. Yeah, I'm after perfection in taste.

I'm a messy, rustic, creative cook with an appreciation for approximation, but that doesn't necessarily yield the *best* baked goods. No, I had some learning to do. And I did. Listen here: if you can learn the lessons that lead to a great cookie—not overmixing, for instance, or when to add extra butter

> "If you can manage to turn
> your cookies from hockey
> pucks into tender, delightful,
> melt-in-your-mouth treats,
> you've really won."

where needed, and how to give the batter a good chill in the fridge—you'll get to the good stuff where baking is concerned. It will take time to fully get there; experience here *definitely* counts. Lucky for you, I've taken the time (more than two full years of my life!) to find shortcuts and paths around the "baking rules" to aid you in finding your way to that intuition necessary for great baking. Every cookie in this book is a delightful setup for better baking.

I hope you always look at baking cookies through a lens of excitement and enjoyment because the cookie bakers lead the charge for home bakers around the world. Home bakers are the memory makers, the architects of nostalgia who make the world a better place through mixing flour, sugar, butter, and joy.

I've never met anyone who didn't like a cookie. In fact, I'd wager that there aren't even many varieties of cookies people dislike. You've got your on-the-fencers about raisins in their cookies, and there are those who turn up their noses at spicy molasses cookies. But the buttery, chocolaty blondies or triple chocolate lunch box cookies… I bet you've never met a *soul* that doesn't enjoy those. See, cookies are a tiny reminder that life is good. Even if we don't have it all together, we can whip up a batch of cookies. Yeah, we could do that.

PREP TIME
15 minutes

BAKE TIME
10 minutes

YIELD
42 cookies

Peanut Butter Blossoms

Ingredients

1 cup butter, softened

1 cup creamy peanut butter

1 cup granulated sugar

1 cup dark brown sugar

1 teaspoon vanilla extract

½ teaspoon kosher salt or ¼
   teaspoon sea salt

2 eggs

3 cups all-purpose flour

42 unwrapped Hershey's Kisses

Directions

Preheat oven to 350°F. Line two baking sheets with parchment paper. In a stand mixer, with a hand mixer, or by hand, cream the butter, peanut butter, and sugars until light and fluffy.

Add the vanilla and salt. Then add the eggs one at a time. Beat 3 to 4 minutes until the batter becomes pale and fluffy. Make sure to scrape down the sides of the bowl.

Gently fold the flour into the mixture. Roll the dough into tablespoon-sized balls, place 2 inches apart on the prepared baking sheets, and bake 9 to 10 minutes.

Once the cookies are baked, remove from the oven and gently press a chocolate kiss into the center of each cookie. Enjoy!

PREP TIME
10 minutes

CHILL TIME
30 minutes

BAKE TIME
12–14 minutes

YIELD
20–24 cookies*

Monster Cookies

I ate my very first monster cookie way back in my twenties. My Midwestern roommate at the time was a fabulous cook, and she'd make things for me that she had eaten as a child, things I'd never tried before: hot dish, monster cookies, casseroles, and more. She'd make sweet-and-sour meatballs with grape jelly—yes, grape jelly! And they were delicious.

It's beautiful how people from different walks of life sharing regional cuisine can **foster friendship** through this glimpse into their lives growing up. Even just here in America, there are so many regional food delights that I'm only touching the tip of the iceberg here. There is **beauty and bounty** in every corner of every state, and I thrill at each opportunity to experience foods from places I've never visited.

These are a thinner, very buttery version of the monster cookies I had way back when. Enjoy!

Ingredients

1½ cups packed dark brown sugar

1 cup butter, softened

½ cup granulated sugar

2 eggs

⅓ cup crunchy peanut butter

1 tablespoon vanilla extract

½ teaspoon flaky sea salt

1¼ cups quick rolled oats

1¼ cups all-purpose flour

1 cup toasted coconut

⅓ cup rye flour

½ teaspoon baking powder

1 cup mini or regular M&M's

¾ cup semisweet chocolate chips

Directions

In a large bowl, whisk the dark brown sugar, butter, granulated sugar, and eggs together, then add the peanut butter, vanilla, and salt. Mix to combine.

Pour the all-purpose flour, oats, coconut, rye flour, and baking powder into the batter.

Add the M&M's and chocolate chips. Fold to combine.

Put the batter in the fridge for 30 minutes. Preheat oven to 350°F while it chills. Line a baking sheet with parchment paper.

Using a ½-ounce scoop or a tablespoon, scoop the batter onto the prepared baking sheet 2 inches apart. Bake the cookies 12 to 14 minutes.

Remove the cookies from the oven when slightly underdone and allow them to cool on the pan. Serve and enjoy!

* *I overfill my cookie scoops, so leveling off your scoops may yield more cookies.*

PREP TIME
10 minutes

BAKE TIME
12–14 minutes

YIELD
36–42 cakes

Russian Tea Cakes

Ingredients

1 cup butter, softened

2½ cups confectioners' sugar, divided

1 teaspoon vanilla extract

½ teaspoon kosher salt

¼ teaspoon pure almond extract

1¾ cups all-purpose flour

1 cup finely chopped pecans

Directions

Preheat oven to 350°F. Line a baking sheet with parchment paper.

Cream butter and ½ cup confectioners' sugar in a mixer on medium speed until whipped and smooth.

Add the vanilla, salt, and almond extract. Mix to combine. Add the flour and pecans and mix until the batter begins to come together and clump up.

Roll the dough into balls and place 2 inches apart on the prepared baking sheet. Bake 12 to 14 minutes.

Once baked and cooled slightly, roll the warm cookies in the remaining confectioners' sugar. Feel free to double roll them. Enjoy!

PREP TIME
10 minutes

BAKE TIME
12–14 minutes

CHILL TIME
30–45 minutes

YIELD
24–28 cookies

Double Chocolate Lunch Box Cookies

My mom would make each of us kids (six total, cousins included) a tailor-made kitchen-sink version of the traditional chocolate chip cookie. I don't remember if mine were double chocolate, but I'd like to think they were. Our cousin Jeff's cookie was the best. We called them Jeffy cookies, and there were M&M's inside. I'm sure mine was a sophisticated batter with rich dark chocolate, cocoa powder, and two to three kinds of chocolate chips.

Truth be told, when testing this recipe, I had three half-full bags of varying chocolate chips, so it was everybody in the bowl! **Happy accidents in the kitchen are a way of life around here.** If you are ever missing an ingredient, just improvise! These guys *must* be my favorite.

Ingredients

1 cup butter, softened

1 cup granulated sugar

1 cup packed dark brown sugar

2 eggs

1 tablespoon vanilla extract

½ teaspoon kosher salt

1¾ cups all-purpose flour

1½ cups chocolate chips (I used a mixture of 60 percent semisweet chips and 72 percent disks)

¾ cup Dutch process unsweetened cocoa powder

Directions

In a stand mixer, or in a large bowl by hand, mix the soft butter and sugars together. Add the eggs one at a time, then add the vanilla and salt. Mix until it just comes together.

Add the flour, chocolate chips, and cocoa powder. Mix until the flour is fully incorporated, but do not overmix.

Refrigerate 30 to 45 minutes. While the dough rests, preheat oven to 350°F and line a rimmed baking sheet with parchment paper.

Remove the dough from the fridge, generously scoop the dough into balls, roughly a heaping tablespoon, and place 2 inches apart on the prepared baking sheet. Bake 9 cookies to a sheet, 12 to 14 minutes.

Allow to cool on a cooling rack, serve, and enjoy!

PREP TIME
5 minutes

BAKE TIME
10–12 minutes

YIELD
16–18 (1-ounce) macaroons

Coconut Custard Macaroons

Ingredients

- 1 (14-ounce) package sweetened shredded coconut
- 1 (14-ounce) can sweetened condensed milk
- 1 egg
- ½ cup melted butter
- 1 teaspoon vanilla extract
- ¾ teaspoon kosher salt

Directions

Preheat oven to 375°F. Line a baking sheet with parchment paper.

In a large mixing bowl, mix all ingredients until completely mixed. Use a large ice cream scoop to distribute equal portions of the dough onto the prepared baking sheet 2 inches apart.

Bake until all edges and tops of cookies are golden brown, 10 to 12 minutes. Depending on the humidity level in your home, the cookies may need a few additional minutes to bake.

Let the cookies set on the cookie sheet for about 5 minutes—but no more than 20 or they will stick! Transfer to a serving dish or plate to continue cooling. Enjoy!

PREP TIME
10 minutes

BAKE TIME
10–12 minutes

YIELD
20–24 cookies

Jam Dots (Thumbprints)

There may not be a simpler cookie. In fact, of all the cookies I've ever made, these little guys are a favorite. That crisp, buttery snap from the shortbread and the chew from the caramelized jam—**it just doesn't get better than that**! These are a great cookie to roll in chopped nuts, raw sugar, or even cocoa powder!

Ingredients

2 cups all-purpose flour

1 cup butter, softened

1 cup confectioners' sugar

1 teaspoon baking powder

1 teaspoon vanilla extract

1 pinch salt

1 cup of your favorite jam

ROLLING OPTIONS

1 cup chopped pistachios

1 cup finely chopped walnuts

½ cup unsweetened cocoa powder

½ cup raw sugar

Directions

Preheat oven to 350°F. Line a baking sheet with parchment paper.

In a stand mixer, or in a large bowl by hand, mix the flour, butter, sugar, baking powder, vanilla, and salt until it comes together and forms a dough.

Pinch roughly 2-teaspoon–sized portions of dough and roll between your palms to create a nice ball. Roll into your topping choice (optional).

Place onto the prepared baking sheet 2 inches apart and press your thumb into each cookie to make an indent.

Fill the indent you've made with ½ teaspoon jam.

Bake 10 to 12 minutes. Allow to cool on a cooling rack. Enjoy!

Cookie Pro Tip:
Double, or even triple,
the dough, and freeze it
in disks to pull out
all season.

PREP TIME
15 minutes

BAKE TIME
45–55 minutes

YIELD
12–16 cookies

Semolina and Almond Biscotti

Ingredients

1 cup sugar

½ cup melted butter (butter can be
melted for 10–15 seconds in the
microwave)

3 eggs

1 teaspoon vanilla extract

1 pinch salt

2¾ cups all-purpose flour

1 cup sliced almonds

½ cup semolina flour

1 teaspoon baking powder

Optional: 10 ounces dark
chocolate to melt for dipping

Directions

Preheat oven to 325°F. Line a baking sheet with parchment paper.

In a stand mixer, cream the sugar, butter, and eggs until light and creamy, about 2 to 3 minutes.

Add the vanilla and salt. Mix to incorporate.

Add the all-purpose flour, almonds, semolina flour, and baking powder. Mix until well combined, but don't overmix.

Turn the dough out onto the prepared baking sheet. Pat gently to form one long loaf of dough roughly 14 to 16 inches long and 5 to 6 inches wide. Bake 30 minutes.

Remove the loaf from the oven and allow to cool 5 to 6 minutes before using a long knife to cut the loaf gently into 12 to 16 cookies.

Lay each cookie on its side and bake another 20 minutes, flipping the cookies midway through.

Cool completely to achieve that signature crunch. The centers will be a bit soft if eaten warm. These are perfect for dunking in coffee, tea, or hot chocolate!

Optional: Melt the chocolate in the microwave in 30-second bursts and gently dip half of each biscotti into it lengthwise. Flip the biscotti chocolate-side-up onto a sheet tray and allow the chocolate to set.

PREP TIME
15 minutes

CHILL TIME
At least 1 hour

BAKE TIME
10–12 minutes

YIELD
20–24 cookies

Chewy Spiced Molasses Cookies

Ingredients

- 1 cup butter, softened
- 1 cup granulated sugar, plus 1 additional cup for rolling
- 1 cup packed dark brown or muscovado sugar
- 1 egg
- ⅓ cup molasses
- 1 teaspoon vanilla extract
- 2½ cups all-purpose flour
- 1 teaspoon baking soda
- ½ teaspoon cinnamon
- ½ teaspoon ground ginger
- ½ teaspoon salt

Directions

Preheat oven to 375°F. Line a baking sheet with parchment paper.

In a stand mixer, cream the butter and sugars only 2 to 3 minutes.

Add the egg, molasses, and vanilla. Mix well to combine.

Add the flour, baking soda, spices, and salt. Mix until well combined. Cover and refrigerate for a minimum of one hour.

Remove the dough from the fridge and roll into balls roughly 1½ inches in size. Roll each ball through the remaining granulated sugar.

Place 2 inches apart on the prepared baking sheet, and bake for 10 to 12 minutes.

Allow to cool before serving. Enjoy!

...there might just be a
miracle right under our noses.

PREP TIME
10 minutes

BAKE TIME
12–14 minutes

YIELD
2 dozen cookies

Butter Flats

Here's a recipe for a buttery, chewy, perfect weekday cookie that I stumbled upon through a "kitchen accident," if you will. See, I make jam thumbprints every year at Christmastime, and you can find that recipe in these pages (they're delectable). When it came time to photograph the thumbprint cookies for inclusion in this book, I figured since I've made them a thousand times, I could make them from memory.

Well, this time instead of the signature thumbprint, I got these flat cookies. I left them to cool on the pan. Defeat! I thought I'd take a breather and come back and try again later. When I came back, I was going to throw the flat cookies away, but then I tasted one. Brilliant! Flat and buttery, with this incredible chew to them. And wonderful—did I mention wonderful? At first, I thought it was a fail. Now I know it wasn't; **it was a perfect happy accident!**

My dear friend Annie has been battling cancer for some time now. I happened to be heading over to visit her on the day I made this happy accident of a cookie. I brought them along for her and her family to enjoy, and soon they were requesting more of these cookies! Knowing that these little cookies brought a modicum of joy during a heartbreaking time made me happy.

It's funny. Sometimes we set out to do one thing and fail to succeed according to our plan. Although the outcome might initially feel like a disaster, ultimately this "failure" can turn out to be a blessing in disguise. If only we could look at all of life this way. **When things don't go as planned, there might just be a miracle right under our noses.**

Ingredients

1 cup butter, softened
1 cup granulated sugar
¾ cup confectioners' sugar
1 teaspoon vanilla extract
¼ teaspoon kosher or sea salt
1 egg
1¾ cups all-purpose flour, plus
  extra for rolling

Directions

Preheat oven to 350°F. Line a baking sheet with parchment paper.

In a large mixing bowl, mix the butter with the sugars, vanilla, and salt. Once well combined, add the egg and then fold in the flour.

Dip your fingertips into the extra flour and roll the cookie dough into balls, roughly a heaping tablespoon, then place them 2 inches apart on the prepared baking sheet.

Bake 10 to 11 minutes and allow to cool to the touch on the baking sheet before moving to a cooling rack. Enjoy!

PREP TIME
5–10 minutes

BAKE TIME
8–10 minutes

YIELD
16–18 cookies

Sticky Marshmallow Toffee Cookies with Black Hawaiian Sea Salt

Making these cookies was epic: I am an avid experimenter in the baking kitchen, and when my mother came back from a trip to Hawaii with black sea salt in tow, I flipped with joy. Black salt? Yes, crunchy, mineral-rich black salt. It's made by mixing lava charcoal and salt in some fabulous way to create a soft salt that lends a beautiful bite and slow finish to any dish. In honor of the salt craze in the sweets world, these gooey cookies needed just a hint of crunchy salt to be perfect. They are, quite possibly, **one of the best I've ever made**.

Ingredients

1 cup butter, softened

½ cup dark brown sugar

¼ cup granulated sugar

1 teaspoon vanilla extract

2 eggs, room temperature

2¼ cups all-purpose flour

½ teaspoon baking soda

2 cups mini marshmallows

1½ cups chocolate chips

1 tablespoon black Hawaiian sea salt, fleur de sel, or any soft-tasting salt, for sprinkling

Directions

Preheat oven to 350°F. Line baking sheets with parchment paper. (You mustn't skip this step. Hot marshmallow acts like glue, and without the parchment, your cookies will not release properly once cooled.)

In a large bowl, mix the butter, sugars, and vanilla until they just come together. Add the eggs one at a time. Mix until just combined; don't overmix at any point in this cookie game.

Add the flour and baking soda, then mix gently until about halfway combined. Add the marshmallows and chocolate chips and mix—again, just until the dough comes together.

Spoon cookies, about 2 tablespoons of dough each, onto the prepared baking sheet, about 2 inches apart, and bake 8 minutes. (They need no more than 10 minutes of baking, but check at 8.)

Remove, sprinkle with salt, and allow to cool completely on the pan. Due to the cookies' gooey nature, I layer squares of parchment paper between the cookies for storing—if they make it that far! Enjoy!

PREP TIME
10 minutes

BAKE TIME
12–15 minutes

CHILL TIME
2 hours to overnight

YIELD
20–24 cookies

Santa's Whiskers

Ingredients

1½ cups confectioners' sugar

1 cup butter, softened

1 (12-ounce) jar pitted maraschino cherries, strained and stemmed

1 teaspoon vanilla extract

½ teaspoon almond extract

½ teaspoon kosher salt

1¾ cups all-purpose flour

2 cups sweetened shredded coconut

Directions

In a stand mixer, with a hand mixer, or by hand, cream the sugar and butter until light and fluffy.

Add the cherries, vanilla, almond extract, and salt. Mix thoroughly. Fold in the flour and mix until it forms a crumbly but moist dough.

Lay a 16-inch sheet of parchment paper onto the counter. Sprinkle 1 cup of the coconut on the center in a loose rectangle, making sure it does not reach the edge of the parchment. Place the cookie dough on top, flattening a bit with your fingers, and sprinkle the remaining coconut over the top of the dough.

Form the dough into a 12- to 14-inch log, about 3 inches thick. Evenly press the coconut around the log and roll to make the log an even cylinder.

Roll the parchment up with the dough inside and twist the ends. Chill for at least 2 hours or overnight.

Preheat oven to 350°F. Line a baking sheet with parchment paper. Slice cookies in ¼- to ½-inch rounds, place on the prepared baking sheet, about 2 inches apart, and bake 12 to 15 minutes. Allow to cool before serving. Store in an airtight container.

Christmas Cookie Pro Tips: Double, or even triple, the dough, and freeze it in disks to pull out all season.

Keep a little well of flour to rest cookie cutters in before and after cutting to ensure a clean cut.

PREP TIME
10 minutes

BAKE TIME
12–14 minutes

CHILL TIME
30 minutes to overnight

YIELD
2 dozen cookies

Vanilla Bean Sugar Cookies

Forty-four years have come and gone since my father, fresh out of high school, left family and friends to join the army. Every year, his grandma Mac, a constant in his life, would make him Christmas cookies for his birthday on December 16 and mail them to wherever in the world he was stationed. My dad looked forward to that shoebox stuffed with cookies, often broken, sometimes weeks old (if they had traveled overseas). Those cookies meant more to him than any gift ever could. That shoebox from that Scottish woman meant he was loved; they meant that somewhere, no matter what, **she was thinking of him**. It was a piece of his home that he could cherish. She sent cookies to my dad up until she passed away. This year, I'm making my dad a shoebox of cookies. I thought long and hard about what to get the greatest man I've ever known. He came from nothing and has given me so much. We are bombarded with all the tricky new stuff we can buy for one another, but what if the ultimate goal this Christmas was to show love?

Betty Crocker might have written an iconic sugar cookie recipe back in the fifties, but I have perfected it by using real butter, farm-fresh eggs, and a healthy dose of real vanilla beans. Christmas cookies are sacred in our home for all they represent. I can remember spreading tinfoil over our entire kitchen table and baking quadruple batches when I was growing up. They would always have messy, pastel cream-cheese icing and needed an overnight open-air cure to make sure they were cakey and not crisp before being stored. No one wants a crispy sugar cookie. Sugar cookies mean far more than jingle bells and twinkly lights. I feel like the simple sugar cookie is a gesture of goodwill. I don't know of any family that doesn't share a cookie around the holidays. These are the cookies to end the year on a hopeful note, reflecting on all that's happened and looking forward to what is to come.

Ingredients

COOKIES

1½ cups confectioners' sugar

1 cup butter, softened

2 tablespoons cream cheese, softened

1 egg

Seeds scraped from one vanilla bean

1 teaspoon almond extract

1 teaspoon salt

2½ cups all-purpose flour

1 teaspoon cream of tartar

Directions

In a stand mixer, with a hand mixer, or by hand, cream the sugar, butter, and cream cheese, together in a large mixing bowl until light and fluffy, about 3 minutes; add the egg, vanilla, almond extract, and salt; mix well.

Add the flour and cream of tartar, and mix by hand until it just comes together. Refrigerate the dough for at least 30 minutes, but overnight is best.

When you are ready to bake, preheat oven to 350°F and line two baking sheets with parchment paper. Roll the dough on a floured surface into a ¼-inch-thick rough circle and use your favorite cookie cutter to cut out shapes.

Christmas Cookie Pro Tips:
Bake cookies only in the top two racks of the oven to prevent an overcooked bottom.

Skip the frosting and mix in dried fruit, chocolate, coconut, or nuts.

CREAM CHEESE FROSTING
1 cup butter, softened
1 (8-ounce) package cream
   cheese, softened
1 teaspoon almond extract
1 pinch salt
4–6 cups confectioners' sugar

Place them on the prepared baking sheet, about 2 inches apart. Bake 12 to 14 minutes, until set.

Continue this process until you've used up all the dough. Cool cookies on sheets of foil and frost once completely cool. These cookies are fine to eat right away, but I think they get their signature touch when frosted and left out overnight. We don't put them away until the next morning.

For the frosting, cream the butter, cream cheese, almond extract, and salt until light and fluffy; slowly add the confectioners' sugar. I like mine less sweet, so I use 4 cups of confectioners' sugar, but you may use up to 6 cups. Feel free to color small bowls of the frosting and decorate the cookies with sprinkles or tiny candies.

My mom stored cookies in a cookie jar just like this one when I was growing up. The original is long gone, but I found the very same one while thrifting, and it's a prized possession.

PREP TIME
15 minutes

BAKE TIME
12–14 minutes

YIELD
20–24 cookies

Perfect Apricot and Chocolate Chunk Oatmeal Cookies

The best cookies are easy drop cookies: warm and gooey with the right amount of chew. Stand mixers are wonderful, but I like a good ol' hand mixer for these cookies!

Ingredients

2 cups dark brown sugar

1 cup butter, softened

1 tablespoon vanilla extract

1 teaspoon kosher salt

2 eggs

2¼ cups rolled oats

1¼ cups all-purpose flour

1 cup dark chocolate chunks

¾ cup diced dried apricots

¾ cup chopped and toasted
    pecans or hazelnuts

Directions

Preheat oven to 350°F. Line a baking sheet with parchment paper.

In a large bowl, mix the sugar, butter, vanilla, and salt, then add the eggs one at a time, mixing slightly after each addition.

Add the oats, flour, chocolate, apricots, and nuts. Mix until just combined.

Drop 6 to 8 large round spoonfuls of dough onto the prepared baking sheet, 2 inches apart.

Bake 12 minutes. The cookies might still be a touch glossy in the center, with golden edges. Bake 1 or 2 additional minutes if they need a bit more browning.

Allow to cool at least 5 to 7 minutes on the cookie sheet before placing them to cool on wire racks. Enjoy!

PREP TIME
10 minutes

BAKE TIME
10–12 minutes

YIELD
2 dozen cookies

Gloria's Chocolate Drops with Cream Cheese Glaze

My grandmother turns eighty-five this year. I called her recently and said, "Grammy, I'd love to make those cookies you made for everything when we were growing up. They were my favorite!" She said she'd look for the recipe.

A few hours later she called and said, "Well, I have it, honey, but it's not mine. It came from a *Good Housekeeping* cookbook published in 1980. I've changed a few things here and there, but I don't think you can put it in your book!"

I said, "Well, read me through it, Grammy. Let's see if you've changed it enough." Sure enough, she had. We do vanilla icing, add a bit of cream cheese, and use cocoa powder instead of melted chocolate. I've added more butter too, because why not. I think we've improved on the memories I had when I was a child.

It has taken on a life of its own. You see, **recipes follow us, ever changing**, adapting and adaptable.

Ingredients

COOKIES

1 cup granulated sugar

¾ cup butter, softened

1 egg

2 cups all-purpose flour

2 tablespoons cocoa powder

1 teaspoon vanilla extract

½ teaspoon baking soda

½ teaspoon salt

½ cup milk

FROSTING

1½ cups confectioners' sugar

4 ounces cream cheese, softened

¼ cup butter, softened

⅓ teaspoon salt

Splash of milk

Directions

Preheat oven to 350°F. Line a baking sheet with parchment paper.

In a large mixing bowl, cream the sugar and butter 2 to 3 minutes, then add the egg and continue mixing.

Add the flour, cocoa powder, vanilla, baking soda, and salt. While mixing, add the milk.

Drop tablespoon-size dollops of dough onto the prepared baking sheet 2 inches apart.

Bake 10 to 12 minutes and cool completely.

For the frosting, in a mixing bowl, combine all ingredients and whip until smooth, then frost each cooled cookie. Enjoy!

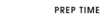
PREP TIME
15 minutes, plus optional 1 hour chill
time and 30 minutes stand time

BAKE TIME
11–15 minutes

YIELD
2 dozen cookies

The Ultimate Rye Chocolate Chip Cookie

This cookie, gosh, is really setting the bar as the perfect cookie. I love puddles of chocolate in a cookie, but I also want to really appreciate the buttery, gooey blond cookie dough at the same time.

Rye flour is nutty and dark; it's like wheat flour's sophisticated older sister. Rye is ground from rye berries, grains that grow on rye grass. It's soft, a far cry from the grittiness wheat flour sometimes offers in a chocolate chip cookie.

Now, I'm always up for a solid chocolate chip cookie recipe, and sometimes I want a little extra nutritional value in my cookies. Okay, okay, maybe not that, but I do love the nutty texture the rye adds, and rye flour is so good for you! When paired with dark chocolate (also a health powerhouse), we are basically eating salad! So go on—brown that butter and enjoy one or three, because these are the perfect crispy, chewy, nutty, buttery chocolate cookies of your dreams…with some good stuff in there too.

Ingredients

1 cup salted butter
1 cup packed dark brown sugar
1 cup granulated sugar
½ teaspoon kosher salt
2 eggs, room temperature
1 tablespoon vanilla extract
1¼ cups all-purpose flour
1 cup rye flour
½ cup dark chocolate disks, chips, or chopped chunks (from your favorite chocolate bar)

Directions

In a medium saucepan, brown the butter over medium to medium-high heat. Swirl constantly 5 to 7 minutes until the butter turns a rich golden brown.

Pour into a large bowl and allow to cool to room temperature. This is important as too much heat will toughen the final cookie texture. Mix the room-temperature brown butter with the sugars and salt.

Add the eggs and vanilla. Mix.

Add the flours and gently mix, then add the chocolate. Do not overmix.

Refrigerate the dough for about 1 hour. You can skip this step, but I love it because it helps to hydrate the dough and marry the flavors. If you skip it, the cookies will spread a bit more instead of holding that large bakery-style cookie texture.

Remove the dough from the fridge and let stand 30 minutes. Preheat oven to 350°F. Line a baking sheet with parchment paper. Scoop dough balls the size of a heaping tablespoon onto the prepared baking sheet, about 2 inches apart.

Bake 13 to 15 minutes. I suggest setting a timer for 11 minutes and checking the cookies every minute or so after.

PREP TIME
10 minutes

BAKE TIME
12 minutes

YIELD
32 cookies

Hummingbird Oatmeal Cookies

Ingredients

1 cup butter, softened

1 cup dark brown sugar

¾ cup granulated sugar

2 eggs

2 teaspoons vanilla extract

1 heaping cup oats (I used
   Quaker Quick Oats)

1 cup flour

1 cup sweetened shredded
   coconut

1 cup chopped walnuts

1 cup golden raisins or chopped,
   dried pineapple

¾ teaspoon cinnamon

¾ teaspoon baking powder

¾ teaspoon kosher salt

Directions

Preheat oven to 350°F. Line a baking sheet with parchment paper.

In a mixer, cream the butter and sugars until fluffy, then add the eggs one at a time. Stream in the vanilla. Add the remaining ingredients and mix until just combined.

Scoop ½-ounce portions (a hefty walnut-in-the-shell size) and pop them onto the prepared baking sheet about 2 inches apart. Bake 12 minutes or until the gloss leaves the top of the cookie and the edges are slightly golden.

Slide the entire parchment out onto the counter or kitchen table to cool. Repeat the process. Try to not eat these all at once!

PREP TIME
15 minutes

BAKE TIME
10–12 minutes

YIELD
12–16 sandwiches

Peanut Butter and Ganache Cookie Sandwiches

Ingredients

¾ cup peanut butter

½ cup butter, softened

1 cup dark brown sugar

½ cup granulated sugar

2 eggs

¼ cup molasses

1 teaspoon vanilla extract

½ teaspoon baking soda

½ teaspoon kosher salt

2½ cups all-purpose flour

GANACHE

1½ cups chocolate chips (your favorite kind)

½ cup heavy cream

½ teaspoon vanilla extract

1 pinch salt

Directions

Preheat oven to 350°F. Line a baking sheet with parchment paper.

In a large bowl, mix the peanut butter, butter, and sugars.

Add the eggs, molasses, vanilla, baking soda, and salt. Mix well.

Add the flour and mix well.

Roll the dough into teaspoon-size balls and place on a parchment-lined baking sheet, about 3 inches apart. Use a fork to press a crosshatch pattern into each ball.

Bake 10 to 12 minutes.

Cool slightly before moving to a wire rack to finish cooling.

Prep the ganache while the cookies bake and cool. Melt the chocolate with the cream over a double boiler or in a small saucepan over medium heat.

Remove from the heat, then add the vanilla extract and salt. Cool completely.

Once the cookies are cooled, sandwich roughly 1 teaspoon of the ganache between two cookies. Enjoy!

PREP TIME
10 minutes

CHILL TIME
15 minutes

BAKE TIME
12 minutes

ASSEMBLY TIME
15 minutes

YIELD
12 big cookies and
6 ice cream sandwiches

Chocolate Chip and Pretzel Cookie Ice Cream Sandwiches

Ingredients

½ cup plus 1 tablespoon butter, softened

½ cup packed dark brown sugar

½ cup granulated sugar

1 egg

1 teaspoon vanilla extract

¼ teaspoon kosher salt

1¼ cups all-purpose flour

½ cup dark chocolate chips

½ cup chopped pretzels

½ teaspoon baking soda

1 pint (2 cups) vanilla ice cream

Directions

Preheat oven to 375°F. Line a baking sheet with parchment paper.

In a large bowl, mix the butter and sugars until creamy.

Add the egg, vanilla, and salt. Mix.

Add the flour, chocolate chips, pretzels, and baking soda. Mix well and refrigerate 15 to 20 minutes.

Scoop 12 even scoops of dough onto the prepared baking sheet, about 2 inches apart.

Bake 12 minutes and allow to cool. Once cooled, scoop ¼ cup softened vanilla ice cream onto the underside of half of the cookies, then top with another cookie, making 6 sandwiches. Enjoy!

PREP TIME
10 minutes

BAKE TIME
12 minutes

YIELD
12–14 sandwiches

Sprinkle Shortbread Cookie Sammies

I'm not sure if there is anything that brings as much joy as **sprinkles and butter**. This buttery, delicate, *deliciously* pink butter cream-filled double disks of happiness should be on your shortlist of simple, fabulous cookies that make people smile.

Ingredients

COOKIE

2 cups flour

1 cup confectioners' sugar

1 cup soft butter

½ cup rainbow sprinkles

1 teaspoon baking powder

1 teaspoon vanilla

Pinch of salt

PINK BUTTERCREAM

3 cups confectioners' sugar

1 cup soft butter

4 ounces soft cream cheese

2 tablespoons heavy cream

2–3 drops red food coloring OR
   ½ cup freeze dried strawberry
   powder

Pinch of salt

Directions

Mix up the cookie ingredients in the work bowl of your stand mixer or mix by hand.

Dump the dough out onto plastic wrap and, gently using the plastic wrap, shape the dough into a log roughly 10 to 12 inches long and 2 inches wide.

Seal the edges of the plastic wrap and roll on the counter to compress and form the dough tube. Refrigerate 2 hours.

Once it's time to bake, preheat oven to 350°F. Unroll the cookies and slice into ¼-inch discs.

Place the disks onto a parchment-lined baking sheet and bake 10 to 12 minutes. Cool completely before filling with pink buttercream.

For the buttercream, cream together the confectioners' sugar, soft butter, cream cheese, and heavy cream.

Add the food coloring or strawberry powder. Mix.

Fill the cooled shortbread round with a teaspoon or 2 of frosting, then place another on top to create a sandwich.

Puddings, Possets, and Panna Cotta

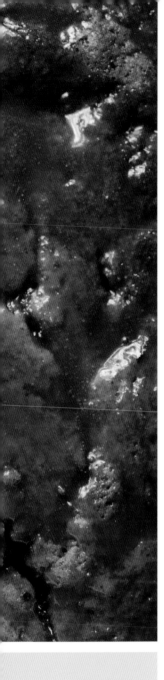

YOUR FIRST LOVE

Gone are the days of peel-top pudding cups (though, admittedly, these lunch box treasures do still hold a magical place in my heart). Enter now into rich, creamy chocolate budino thickened with egg yolk. Behold smooth, delicious farina with berries, swirls of heavy cream, and a surface dotted with butter and whimsy.

Pudding is probably the first dessert you learned to love. Because of its velvety smoothness, it's often the first sweet offered to babies and small children. It's the stuff you've come to love, and I know for me it holds a wild nostalgia.

When I was a kid, my siblings and I would whip up a box of Jell-O pudding cook-and-serve (almost never instant) and eagerly divide the pudding we'd cooked into six glasses. My mom had these vintage jelly jars we used almost exclusively for eating pudding. We relished the whole experience. The skin that formed on the top of the pudding was a chewy treat that ushered you into the pudding cup. To enjoy the spoils of our labor, my family would flop in front of the TV to watch some special program on a Friday night.

Pudding is the sweet we kids made. My mother made tapioca, but my brothers and sister and I did the pudding. You'll notice in these recipes that I never ask you to lay a plastic film across pudding to keep a skin from forming. For me, that's the best part! I'll never cover a pastry cream with plastic wrap. If I'm really worried it'll change the texture too much, I'll just secretly skim off the top and place it in a bowl as a cook's treat. It was my dad's favorite part of the pudding when he was a child, and he handed that love down.

The recipes in this chapter are all about whimsy and true love. They are about childhood and real life. The posset clings to the bits of motherhood you simply cannot hold on to, though onward they march. Pudding should be put back into your routine. Welcome these creamy dreams back into the spotlight of your weeknight sweet rotation. You won't be sorry.

PREP TIME
10 minutes

COOK TIME
10 minutes

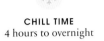
CHILL TIME
4 hours to overnight

YIELD
4–6 servings

Creamy Dark Chocolate Budino

When I was growing up, my dad loved to cook and serve puddings, and we never, under any circumstances, placed plastic wrap over the tops of puddings to prevent the skin from forming. My dad *loved* the skin, so naturally **I became really fond of it too.** To this day I don't cover a pastry cream or pudding, and I don't mind that chewy extra bit of texture the skin of the pudding provides.

Ingredients

1 cup sugar

½ cup unsweetened cocoa powder

½ cup dark chocolate (your favorite chocolate chips work great)

¼ cup cornstarch

1 pinch salt

3 egg yolks

2½ cups whole milk

1 cup heavy cream

1 tablespoon butter

1 teaspoon vanilla extract

SOFT WHIPPED CREAM

2 cups heavy cream

2 heaping tablespoons confectioners' sugar

Splash of vanilla extract

Directions

In a saucepan over medium heat, combine the sugar, cocoa powder, chocolate, cornstarch, and salt.

Whisk the egg yolks into the milk and cream, then slowly stream into the chocolate mixture.

Whisk continually until it thickens but does not boil, 5 to 6 minutes. Turn off the heat and set aside.

Add the butter and vanilla. Stir until glossy and well combined.

Pour into a 2-quart bowl and refrigerate 4 hours or overnight.

When it's time to serve, scoop the pudding into individual bowls.

For the whipped cream, using a hand or stand mixer, mix the ingredients on medium speed until soft peaks form, then serve alongside the pudding. Enjoy!

COOK TIME
20 minutes

CHILL TIME
4–24 hours

YIELD
6 servings

Old-Fashioned Butterscotch Pudding

Ingredients

1 cup dark brown sugar

⅛–¼ cup tepid water

4 cups heavy whipping cream

2 pinches sea salt, divided

4 egg yolks

1 whole egg

2–3 tablespoons rye whiskey
(optional)

CREAM CARAMEL TOPPING

1½ cups granulated sugar

4 tablespoons butter

½ cup heavy cream

1 pinch of salt

Directions

Select 6 dessert glasses or cups to hold your cooked pudding. In a heavy-bottom saucepan, heat the brown sugar and water over medium to medium-high heat until it bubbles. This creates a quick caramel.

Slowly whisk in the heavy cream and a pinch of salt. Reduce the heat to medium, then stir constantly until the mixture begins to simmer but do not boil.

In a separate bowl, whisk the 4 egg yolks along with the whole egg.

Gently ladle 1 cup of the hot cream mixture into the eggs while whisking vigorously. This is called tempering your eggs.

Then, slowly stream the eggs back into the cream pot. Whisk 8 to 10 minutes, until the pudding thickens.

Turn off the heat and flavor with the whiskey to taste. Add the remaining pinch of sea salt. Let stand 10 minutes before filling the dessert glasses. You can get up to 10 servings by choosing smaller serving vessels.

Ladle the pudding evenly among the glasses and refrigerate at least 4 hours. Cover each pudding with plastic wrap to prevent fridge smells from scenting it.

For the cream caramel, add the sugar and ⅛ cup water to a small, heavy-bottom saucepan. Cook over medium heat until it begins to turn a deep amber color. Do not stir the sugar as it cooks, or it may crystallize.

Once the sugar turns amber in color, remove the saucepan from the heat and add the butter. Whisk until the butter is incorporated.

Add the heavy cream and stir until smooth. It will hiss and sputter a bit. Add a pinch of salt, then cool completely before topping the puddings. Enjoy!

PREP TIME
5 minutes

COOK TIME
5–7 minutes

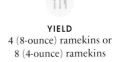
YIELD
4 (8-ounce) ramekins or
8 (4-ounce) ramekins

Creamy Lemon and Vanilla Bean Posset

"Mom, can I try the creams you are making for photos? The little lemon opossums?"

It was 7:00 a.m. and Noah came into my room so excited to try yesterday's shoot creation. He absolutely loved them. He doesn't mispronounce much these days; he's just too big for that. But on this glorious morning he called the puddings "**lemon opossums**." I said, "It's posset, silly!" We laughed and he ran away.

Is it wrong to **savor** every bit of him little? He's growing so fast and changing like lightning, a boy knocking on the door of being a man. Ten is an age where he has a foot in both worlds. Motherhood is a constant exercise in letting go and looking forward. I'll gleefully hold on to every shred of the small boy he's leaving behind. I think I might just call these treats lemon opossums forever—to remind me to slow down and take life in. **To truly savor simple moments** in raising young men.

This little lemon posset, much like raising kids, is truly a miracle. It's so easy to ruin custard (too much heat, curdling, breaking). But this pudding comes together so quickly and simply it feels foolproof. Its light, creamy lemon goodness reminds me of the wonderful things to come and all there is to love about the past. Memories can be bittersweet, soft, and comforting, sure, but also a tart reminder that they are times gone. I'll savor every bit.

Thank you to Britain for bringing us the posset. And thank you, Noah, for **making me a mom**.

Ingredients

- ⅓ cup freshly squeezed lemon juice (roughly 2 juicy lemons)
- 3 cups heavy whipping cream
- 1 shy cup sugar (shy meaning barely full)
- 1 vanilla bean, split and scraped (if available), or 1 teaspoon vanilla extract
- Fresh raspberries, mint, and whipped cream for garnish

Directions

Squeeze lemon juice into a measuring cup and set aside.

In a medium saucepan, bring the cream, sugar, and vanilla to a boil over medium-high heat. After 4 to 5 minutes, remove from the heat, making sure the cream doesn't boil over. It may want to!

Add the lemon juice and stir. Pour into your preferred ramekins and allow to cool completely.

Refrigerate at least 4 hours or overnight. (I like these best overnight!) Garnish with the berries, mint, and whipped cream. Serve and enjoy!

PREP/COOK TIME
20 minutes

CHILL TIME
4–24 hours

YIELD
6–8 (4-ounce) servings

Swedish Cream with Port Wine and Berries

Growing up, there was just one tiny fancy restaurant nearby: Marzano. This little Italian place first introduced me to the wonders of dipping crusty baguettes in olive oil and finely grated Grana Padano. I celebrated birthdays and homecomings there. Marzano was one of the reasons I opened my own restaurant. It's been there nearly 30 years, and it feels sort of like home when I walk through the doors of that tiny, converted house.

I've tried most of my life to replicate Marzano's delicate Swedish cream. They still make it to this day. After decades, **nothing has changed**. Port wine and fresh berries. It's magical. And this recipe is as close as I can get to it without knowing exactly just what magic makes up theirs. But it's delightful. Enjoy!

Ingredients

SWEDISH CREAM

2 cups heavy cream

1 cup whole milk

½ cup sugar

1 pinch salt

1 envelope gelatin

1 teaspoon vanilla bean paste
  (or vanilla extract)

4 ounces cream cheese, softened

½ cup sour cream

Directions

Bring the cream, milk, sugar, and salt to a simmer in a medium saucepan over medium heat, but do not boil.

Meanwhile, bloom the envelope of gelatin in 2 to 3 tablespoons of water by whisking together with a fork. The gelatin should have the consistency of applesauce. Allow to stand 2 to 3 minutes.

Whisk the bloomed gelatin into the cream mixture and continue whisking to dissolve completely. Remove from the heat and add the vanilla.

Mix together the cream cheese and sour cream in a bowl. Then, slowly pour the gelatin-cream mixture over the cream cheese and sour cream in ½-cup increments. By doing this slowly, you can avoid lumps. Cool 10 minutes.

Divide evenly among 6 to 8 glasses or ramekins. Chill 4 hours at least, up to 24 hours.

PORT WINE AND BERRIES

2 pints fresh raspberries

2 pints fresh blueberries

8 ounces or 1 cup ruby port wine

½ cup sugar

Lemon juice

For the port wine and berries, bring 1 pint of raspberries, 1 pint of blueberries, wine, sugar, and lemon juice to a simmer in a saucepan over medium heat. Smash the berries with a fork. Simmer 10 minutes.

Press the sauce through a fine mesh sieve, then place in a bowl to cool completely in the fridge. Discard the pulp.

When it's time to serve, spoon the strained sauce over the cream and top with remaining fresh berries. Enjoy!

PREP TIME
10 minutes

COOK TIME
10 minutes

YIELD
6 just over servings
(½ cup each)

Real Pistachio Pudding

Ingredients

1½ cups shelled pistachios

Pinch of salt

1 cup sugar

2½ cup heavy cream

1 cup milk

3 egg yolks

1 tablespoon cornstarch

2 tablespoons butter

1 teaspoon vanilla extract

Whipped cream and chopped
salted pistachios, for serving

Directions

In a food processor, whirl the pistachios until they begin to clump up, about 2 to 3 minutes.

Add the salt, sugar, and ½ cup heavy cream. Continue to blend until it forms a smooth paste.

Transfer the paste to a medium-sized saucepan and add the remaining heavy cream and milk. Whisk gently to combine.

Bring to a simmer over medium heat; do not boil. Stir continually.

Meanwhile, in a mixing bowl, whisk the egg yolks well with the cornstarch. Begin to ladle the hot cream mixture into the eggs, whisking constantly to temper the eggs. Pour the tempered egg mixture back into the simmering cream and stir 5 to 6 minutes until it thickens slightly.

Remove from the heat and add the butter and vanilla. Stir to combine.

Pour into 6 small cups, or 4 larger cups, and chill for 4 hours. Top with extra whipped cream and chopped salted pistachios.

PREP TIME
5 minutes

BAKE TIME
60–80 minutes

YIELD
6–8 (4-ounce) servings

CHILL TIME
4–24 hours

Old School Tapioca Cream Pudding with Rhubarb Compote

Ingredients

TAPIOCA PUDDING

3 cups whole milk

1¼ cups heavy cream

2 eggs

⅔ cup sugar

½ cup plus 1 tablespoon tapioca
    pearls (not instant)

1 pinch salt

2 teaspoons vanilla extract

⅓ cup heavy cream

RHUBARB COMPOTE

3 cups rhubarb (2 stalks)

1 cup sugar

Juice of half a lemon

Directions

Whisk the milk, cream, eggs, sugar, tapioca, and salt, then bring to a simmer (but do not boil) in a saucepan over medium-low heat. Stir continually and simmer 60 to 80 minutes.

Remove from heat and add the vanilla extract.

Allow to stand 10 minutes, then stir in heavy cream.

Place into a serving bowl, or bowls, and place in the refrigerator.

For the rhubarb compote, wash and prepare the rhubarb by slicing it on the bias (diagonally) into ¼-inch-thick slices.

Bring the rhubarb, sugar, 1 cup water, and lemon juice to a simmer in a saucepan over medium heat. Cook until the rhubarb is tender and the syrup has thickened slightly, no more than 15 to 20 minutes.*

Cool completely and store in the fridge in glass jars. Keeps for up to 1 week.

To serve, spoon the pudding into serving dishes and top with syrup and whipped cream. Enjoy!

* *This may vary depending on how young your rhubarb is. Fresh rhubarb will be tender in approximately 7 to 10 minutes. More mature stalks may take longer.*

PREP TIME
20 minutes

BAKE TIME
35–40 minutes

YIELD
1 (9-inch) cake

Sticky Toffee Pudding

Frozen nights and early evenings call for a **revamped classic**. The self-saucing pudding is quite the rage in Great Britain, and I think for a good reason: tender cake with the perfect amount of goo at the bottom! I am a huge fan of even more butterscotch goodness, so I opted for a pouring toffee sauce as well. Add a creamy scoop of vanilla ice cream and you've got a spiced, warm dessert that rivals all others—and might **remind you of your grandma** in the best way possible. A perfect winter treat dish so easy, you can enjoy it midweek!

Ingredients

1½ cups pitted, dried dates

¾ cup unsweetened apple juice

2 cups dark brown sugar, divided

½ cup granulated sugar

½ cup plus 3 tablespoons butter,
    softened and divided

3 eggs

1 teaspoon salt

1 teaspoon vanilla extract

1 teaspoon pumpkin pie spice

½ teaspoon cinnamon

1¼ cups all-purpose flour

1 teaspoon baking powder

1 teaspoon baking soda

1 cup boiling water

Heavy cream, for garnish

Vanilla ice cream, for serving
    (optional)

Directions

Preheat oven to 350°F. Generously butter a 9-by-9-inch baking dish; set aside.

Bring the dates and apple juice to a boil in a medium saucepan over medium-high heat, carefully smashing with a fork; cover and remove from heat.

Meanwhile, in a large mixing bowl, mix 1 cup dark brown sugar, the granulated sugar, ½ cup of butter until well combined; add the eggs one at a time and mix until well incorporated.

Add the salt, vanilla, and spices. Fold in the flour, baking powder, and baking soda until just mixed.

Add the hot date mixture with the mixer running on low.

Spoon the cake batter into the prepared baking dish. Dot the top of the cake with the remaining softened butter, and sprinkle the remaining 1 cup dark brown sugar over that.

Pour the boiling water over the top of the cake (I use the dirty date pan to bring water to a boil) and bake 25 to 30 minutes or until the cake has set and the top has crackled slightly. Allow to cool at least 10 minutes before scooping to serve.

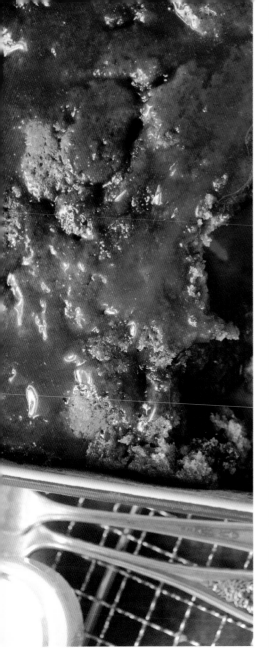

EXTRA TOFFEE SAUCE

1 cup dark brown sugar

¾ cup heavy cream

1 pinch salt

For the toffee sauce, cook the brown sugar and cream together in a saucepan over medium heat until the sugar dissolves, about 3 to 4 minutes, and add the salt.

To serve, spoon out the heavenly pudding and drizzle a bit of sauce and heavy cream over the top. Serve with vanilla ice cream or by itself. It's something your family will enjoy for years to come. Enjoy!

PREP TIME
15 minutes

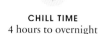
CHILL TIME
4 hours to overnight

YIELD
1 (9-by-13-inch) dish

Irish Cream Tiramisu

Ingredients

2 (8-ounce) packages cream
    cheese, softened

3 cups heavy whipping cream

⅓ cup Irish cream liqueur

½–¾ cup dark brown sugar
    (depending on how sweet you
    prefer it; start with ½ cup)

1 teaspoon vanilla extract

1 pinch salt

A touch of milk to thin, if needed

COFFEE SOAK

3 cups strong coffee or espresso*

2 tablespoons light brown sugar

1 tablespoon instant coffee
    granules

1 tablespoon vanilla extract

1 pinch kosher salt

2 (7-ounce) packages ladyfinger
    cookies

½ cup unsweetened cocoa
    powder

Directions

Beat the soft cream cheese for 2 minutes on low speed in a stand mixer or with a hand mixer.

Slowly add the heavy whipping cream while the mixer is on and increase the speed to medium.

Scrape down the sides of the bowl and slowly pour the Irish cream liqueur into the cream mixture.

Add the brown sugar, vanilla extract, and salt. Mix. The cream should feel like thick whipped cream and slightly hold its shape when spooned. If needed, thin with some cream. Set aside.

For the coffee soak, combine the coffee, brown sugar, coffee granules, vanilla extract, and salt in a wide and shallow bowl. Unwrap the ladyfingers and quickly lay them into the coffee soak, covering completely. I like to dip, turn, and remove. This should last no more than 2 seconds. Repeat this process and then cover the bottom of a 9-by-13-inch glass dish with the ladyfingers.

Spread half the cream mixture over the top of the cookies. Dust half the cocoa powder on top of the cream.

Repeat, and cover that layer with soaked ladyfinger cookies. Dust the top with the remaining cocoa powder. Chill for at least 4 hours before serving, but overnight is best. Enjoy!

* I love to use store-bought cold brew!

A fast, lovely way...

...to say good night.

PREP TIME
5 minutes

COOK TIME
5 minutes

YIELD
3 cups, roughly 3–4 servings

Farina Porridge

Cream of Wheat: I grew up eating this delight for breakfast, snacks, and sometimes dessert. I remember telling kids at school how much I loved Cream of Wheat. It seemed that nobody ate it with anything more than a touch of butter and brown sugar. Now I make this porridge for my boys on lazy weekend mornings or during the week for a bedtime snack. It's a fast, **lovely way to say good night.**

Ingredients

1 cup milk, plus extra if desired

2 tablespoons butter

1 pinch kosher salt

1 cup farina (Cream of Wheat, Malt-O-Meal, or Bob's Red Mill Creamy Wheat, a personal favorite)

TOPPINGS

1 teaspoon butter

Dark brown sugar

Raspberries

Blueberries

Heavy cream

Chopped walnuts or pecans

Golden raisins

Directions

Bring 2 cups water, milk, butter, and salt to a simmer in a saucepan over medium-high heat.

Whisk in the farina and gently stir 3 to 5 minutes until thickened and creamy. Add an additional splash of milk if you prefer it a bit thinner.

Spoon into bowls and top with a pat of butter, about 1 teaspoon or so.

Top with any toppings you love. I use a tablespoon or two of brown sugar and add berries.

Drizzle with 1 to 2 tablespoons of heavy cream.

PREP TIME
20 minutes

CHILL TIME
4–24 hours

YIELD
6 (4-ounce) portions

Passion Fruit Panna Cotta

Ingredients

2 cups heavy cream

1 cup whole milk

½ cup sugar

1 pinch salt

1 envelope gelatin

1 cup passion fruit pulp, divided

Directions

Bring the cream, milk, sugar, and salt to a simmer in a medium saucepan over medium heat, but do not boil.

Meanwhile, bloom the envelope of gelatin in 2 to 3 tablespoons of water by whisking together with a fork. Allow to stand 2 to 3 minutes.

Whisk the bloomed gelatin into the cream mixture, then whisk to dissolve completely. Add ½ cup of the passion fruit pulp. Remove from heat. Cool 10 minutes.

Divide evenly among 6 glasses or ramekins. Chill at least 4 hours or up to 24 hours.

When it's time to serve, spoon the remaining passion fruit pulp over the top.

Bars and Bakes

PRAYIN' FOLKS

We've all experienced, in some way or another, a recipe—maybe it was your grandmother's or a friend's great-aunt's recipe—so wildly delicious that it leaves you saying, "Wow! What a treat! Can I have the recipe?" What a legacy.

Sometimes, folks who have gone home to heaven get to live on here through their recipes, sharing something of themselves with the family they left behind, perhaps even family they never had the chance to meet while living. Before my grandpa passed away, he spent years making a bound book from magazine clippings, newspapers, and friends titled "Not My Recipes." I found it cute while he was still with us, but now it's more than that—it's special to me.

I think about how my boys, Noah and Milo, will grow up to have children of their own, and those children will grow up, and so on. I happily imagine my grandchildren at Christmas saying, "Here is my grandma's fudge recipe!" Our lives are made up of these moments that leave marks on our hearts forever. I also believe there were profound moments of prayer long before I was born that poured blessings into my life. My greatest gift is that I am living through a legacy passed down from great-grandparents, grandparents, and God-fearing parents. They prayed Jesus into my life, blessings.

Please start praying for your family, for your children. Pray for a legacy of children and family who do good and love the Lord and serve God fiercely. Pray for restoration. Pray without ceasing. Pray that your children and their children's children know that you prayed. The mark on their life will be so undeniable that they will know you stood for a legacy led by prayer. Also, that you made damn good fudge!

There is far more at stake in passing down recipes than we think. Passing down recipes is much more than a novelty. It's a way we can connect to people we might never get to know. We can change the future when we start now. Maybe you don't come from a line of praying folks, or even kind people. You get to change that now for your family. You have an arsenal of recipes to choose from to pray over and start making as a tradition. I pray blessings onto these recipes that the people who make them will create precious memories around them.

I hope you never look over recipes for cookie bars, no-bake cheesecake slabs, and fudge in quite the same way. Who knew making something sweet to celebrate simple things could have such an impact?

PREP TIME
15 minutes

BAKE TIME
30–35 minutes

YIELD
1 (9-by-13-inch) pan

Cream Cheese Blondies

Ingredients

1 cup salted butter

1 cup packed dark brown sugar

½ cup granulated sugar

2 eggs

1 teaspoon kosher salt

1 teaspoon vanilla extract

2 cups all-purpose flour

½ teaspoon baking powder

CREAM CHEESE

1 (8-ounce) package cream
   cheese, softened

1 egg

¼ cup granulated sugar

1 pinch salt

Directions

Preheat oven to 350°F.

Line a 9-by-13-inch baking dish with parchment paper. Melt the butter in a saucepan over medium heat until it begins to foam and brown. Turn the heat off. Allow to cool 5 to 10 minutes.

Meanwhile, mix the sugars and eggs in the bowl of a stand mixer or large mixing bowl (by hand or with a hand mixer) for 5 to 7 minutes. Slowly stream in the warm butter, salt, and vanilla. Add the flour and baking powder and mix until just combined. Set the dough aside.

For the cream cheese, in another bowl, mix the softened cream cheese and egg with the sugar until the mixture is silky smooth with no lumps. Press ⅔ of the dough into the prepared pan. Pour the cream cheese mixture over the top of the dough and press the last ⅓ of the dough over top of the cream cheese.

Bake 30 to 35 minutes or until just set. You want to remove the blondies from the oven before they are 100 percent cooked through. Cool 10 minutes before slicing.

Serve and enjoy.

PREP TIME
10 minutes

BAKE TIME
25–27 minutes

YIELD
9–10 muffins

Classic and Tender Blueberry Muffins

Ingredients

2 eggs

1½ cups granulated sugar

1 cup milk/lemon juice
   combination (3 tablespoons
   lemon juice plus milk, all
   equaling 1 cup)

½ cup melted butter, cooled

2 teaspoons vanilla extract

½ teaspoon kosher salt

Zest of 1 lemon

2¼ cups all-purpose flour, plus
   additional 1 tablespoon for
   sprinkling

1 tablespoon baking powder

2 cups fresh or frozen blueberries

Sparkling or raw sugar for the tops

Directions

Preheat oven to 400°F. Line a jumbo muffin tin with paper liners.

Mix together the eggs, granulated sugar, milk/lemon juice combination, butter, vanilla, salt, and lemon zest.

Add the flour and baking powder, then gently mix.

Add the blueberries, then sprinkle the additional tablespoon flour over the top of the blueberries. Gently mix to combine.

Scoop the dough into the prepared muffin tin. Sprinkle each muffin with sparkling or raw sugar. (This gives the top that signature bakery-style texture and flavor.)

Bake 15 minutes, then decrease the oven temperature to 350° to finish baking, another 10 to 12 minutes.

Serve and enjoy.

PREP TIME
10 minutes

BAKE TIME
20–25 minutes

YIELD
1 (9-by-9-inch) pan

Grasshopper (Slice) Brownies

Ingredients

2 cups granulated sugar

½ cup melted butter, slightly
    cooled

½ cup neutral oil suitable for
    baking

4 eggs

2 teaspoons vanilla extract

1 cup melted bittersweet
    chocolate

1 cup all-purpose flour

½ cup unsweetened cocoa
    powder

½ teaspoon kosher salt

MINT BUTTERCREAM

3–4 cups confectioners' sugar

1 cup butter, softened

2–4 tablespoons heavy cream

½ teaspoon peppermint extract
    (increase if you prefer it more
    minty)

7–10 drops green food coloring
    (optional)

MINT GANACHE

1 cup dark or bittersweet
    chocolate (chocolate chips
    work beautifully)

½ cup heavy cream

1 teaspoon peppermint extract

Directions

Preheat oven to 350°F. Line a 9-by-9-inch square metal baking pan with parchment paper.

In a large mixing bowl, gently mix the granulated sugar, melted butter, oil, eggs, and vanilla. Fold in the melted chocolate.

Fold the flour, cocoa powder, and salt into the batter. Then pour the batter into the prepared baking pan.

Bake 20 to 25 minutes. Do not overbake; this is a gooey brownie.

Allow to cool completely before frosting.

For the buttercream, using a hand mixer or stand mixer, mix the confectioners' sugar, butter, and cream. Once smooth and well combined, add the peppermint extract and food coloring (optional). Spread on the cooled brownies.

For the ganache, melt the chocolate and cream in a small saucepan over medium-low heat. Remove from the heat once the chocolate is almost fully melted. Continue to stir until it's silky smooth, then add the peppermint extract.

Allow to cool to room temperature, then pour over the frosted brownies. This is where you can choose your own adventure! Serve with gooey ganache that hasn't set or pop them in the fridge for a perfect slice once the ganache has set. Either way has its charm! Enjoy!

PREP TIME
15 minutes

BAKE TIME
24–28 minutes

YIELD
1 (9-by-13-inch) pan

Snickerdoodle Bars

Years ago, my husband and I lived in a little apartment where we were just trying to make sense of our lives after having to close our restaurant. We had a small dining room table with only four chairs, so when we would invite more than a couple people over, it was always standing room only for the remaining guests. If there were any littles, they'd usually be seated at the table while the adults took to the floor.

I hosted some beautiful dinner parties in that little place while we started over. One evening our friends brought snickerdoodle bars. I'd never heard of such a thing! Think big, thick, chewy butter bars hot out of the oven and served with a scoop of vanilla ice cream. Perfectly crisp edges and a tender middle. I never did get the recipe from that friend, but I did set out to re-create it. I think these are a success!

I learned in that apartment that **you don't need fancy anything** to make food that is incredibly good. Our little electric coil-top range turned out one delight after another (roasted chicken with my homemade chimichurri was my favorite). I could go on, but let's just leave it at this: We were really living in that place. We were healing. Looking back, I'd do anything to revisit that time for just a moment.

Ingredients

1 cup butter, softened
1 cup granulated sugar
¾ cup confectioners' sugar
1 teaspoon vanilla extract
1 teaspoon cinnamon
1 teaspoon cream of tartar
¼ teaspoon kosher or sea salt
2 eggs
2 cups all-purpose flour

CINNAMON SUGAR TOP
2–3 tablespoons raw sugar
1 teaspoon cinnamon
1 pinch salt

Vanilla ice cream, for serving

Directions

Preheat oven to 350°F. In a large mixing bowl, mix the butter and sugars until smooth, then add vanilla, cinnamon, cream of tartar, and salt. Mix.

Add the eggs and mix well, scraping down the bowl's sides.

Add the flour. Mix to combine.

Butter the baking dish and press the dough inside.

For the sugar top, mix the sugar top ingredients, then sprinkle it over the top.

Bake 24 to 28 minutes. Cool slightly and serve warm with vanilla ice cream.

PREP TIME
10 minutes

KNEADING TIME
10 minutes

PROOFING TIME
1 hour 15 minutes

SECOND RISE TIME
20 minutes

BAKE TIME
25–30 minutes

YIELD
12 rolls in 2 (9-by-13-inch) pans

Brioche Cinnamon Rolls with Cream Cheese Toffee Sauce

Ingredients

3 cups all-purpose flour

1 cup warm milk

3 tablespoons honey

2 tablespoons butter, softened

1 egg, room temperature

2 teaspoons active yeast

1 teaspoon kosher salt

BROWN SUGARED PAN

½ cup melted butter

1 cup dark brown sugar

CINNAMON SUGAR MIXTURE

½ cup butter, softened

1 cup dark brown sugar

1 tablespoon cinnamon

CREAM CHEESE TOFFEE SAUCE

1 (8-ounce) package cream
   cheese, softened

1⅓ cups dark brown sugar

¾ cup heavy cream

Directions

This dough recipe can be prepared by hand, in a stand mixer, or in a bread machine on the dough setting. If using a stand mixer, combine all dough ingredients in the work bowl. Using the dough hook attachment, mix/knead 7 to 10 minutes until the dough is smooth and pulls away from the sides of the bowl. If making by hand, knead the dough 7 to 10 minutes using your palms.

Cover the dough with a damp towel and allow to rise in a warm place for 1 hour and 15 minutes.

Punch down the dough and roll to roughly a 16-by-10-inch rectangle on a lightly floured surface.

For the brown sugared pan, line two 9-by-13-inch pans with parchment paper. Pour half the melted butter and the brown sugar evenly into each pan.

For the cinnamon sugar mixture, mix together the butter, brown sugar, and cinnamon in a small bowl. Spread the mixture evenly onto the dough and roll it up tightly, away from yourself. Slice into 12 even rolls.

Preheat oven to 350°F. Lay 6 rolls into the center of each pan and allow to rise 20 minutes. 6. Bake until the rolls are golden and doubled in size, about 25 to 30minutes.

For the cream cheese toffee sauce, place the softened cream cheese in a bowl. In a medium saucepan over medium heat, melt the brown sugar and heavy cream. Bring this syrup to a simmer.

Ladle ¼ cup of the hot syrup into the cream cheese and mix with a hand mixer until smooth. Continue adding in the syrup slowly, mixing after each addition so you get no cream cheese lumps.

Pour the hot toffee sauce over the cinnamon rolls. Enjoy!

PREP TIME
20 minutes

CHILL TIME
4 hours to overnight

YIELD
1 (9-by-13-inch) pan

Aunty Jenny's Sour Cream and Lemon Pie Bars

Did you ever eat those little no-bake Jell-O lemon cream pies when you were young? The cheesecake kind with that powdery, impossible graham cracker crust? They still make 'em. I loved them as a kid! And I thought, gosh, what if I could get by without the box mix and premade graham crust?

Enter this beautiful slab of creamy lemon goodness. My sister, Jenny, is my best little friend, and she absolutely loves a tart lemon dessert. She brought this beautiful lemon dessert to our parents' house for a summer dinner one year, and I told her then I'd add those bars to my next book! This is as close as I could get from memory, and it's not half bad. This is perfect for a baby shower or the Fourth of July!

Ingredients

16 ounces lemon Greek yogurt

1 (8-ounce) package cream
  cheese, softened

1 package powdered gelatin

Juice of 2–3 lemons, roughly ½ cup
  (I used Meyer lemons)

Zest of one lemon

1 cup heavy cream

1 cup sour cream

1½ cups confectioners' sugar

Fresh blueberries, for serving

Directions

In a large mixing bowl, or in the bowl of your stand mixer, whisk the yogurt and cream cheese until completely smooth.

Bloom the gelatin in the lemon juice 3 to 4 minutes. It'll start to thicken.

Add the gelatin mixture and zest to the filling mixture. Whisk on medium speed 2 to 3 minutes.

Add the heavy cream and sour cream, then scrape the sides and mix until smooth and creamy.

Add the confectioners' sugar. Mix completely.

For the crust, begin pounding the cookies with a heavy-bottom jar or crushing in a food processor.

Mix the cookie crumbs with the melted butter and press into a 9-by-13-inch glass baking dish.

CRUST

1 (11-ounce) box vanilla wafers

4 tablespoons butter, melted

Pour the prepared filling into the crust and refrigerate at least 4 hours (overnight is best).

Serve with fresh blueberries.

PREP TIME
10 minutes

BAKE TIME
25–35 minutes

YIELD
1 (9-by-13-inch) pan

Coconut Cream Lemon Bars

Ingredients

CRUST

2 cups all-purpose flour

1 cup butter, softened

½ cup sugar

½ teaspoon kosher salt

FILLING

1 (14.5-ounce) can coconut
     cream

2 cups sugar

5 large eggs

1 cup fresh lemon or lime juice
     (I use both)

½ cup all-purpose flour

Zest of 2 lemons (about 2 heaping
     tablespoons)

½ teaspoon pure coconut extract

½ teaspoon kosher salt

1 cup sweetened shredded
     coconut

Directions

Preheat oven to 350°F. In a stand mixer, with a hand mixer, or by hand, mix ingredients for the crust until it comes together. It may be a bit crumbly, and that's okay.

Press into the bottom of a 9-by-13-inch baking dish and bake about 15 minutes, until the top has just begun to show signs of browning.

For the filling, add the coconut cream to a mixing bowl along with the sugar.

Slowly add each egg so you get a smooth, creamy-textured filling with no lumps.

Add lemon juice, flour, lemon zest, coconut extract, and salt.

Mix and pour over baked and slightly cooled crust.

Add shredded coconut to the top or mix it into the filling. Bake 25 to 30 minutes, or until the center has just set and no longer wobbles but has not cracked. Cool and serve.

PREP TIME
20 minutes

CHILL TIME
4 hours to overnight

YIELD
1 (9-by-13-inch) pan

Airforce Easter Custard

My sister, Jenny, lived in Knob Noster, Missouri, for almost eight years, and while there she picked up some beautiful regional recipes. It's been ten years since she moved home to Washington State, and ever since she has made this dessert every Easter. It reminds me of homecomings and chubby babies and wearing your Easter best. It reminds me that we all have a new life now because of Easter, because a savior had been brought back to life. I may love Easter more than Christmas. So make this and remember it just ain't over! **Get back up because this life is sweet!**

Ingredients

WHIPPING CREAM

1 cup heavy cream

2 tablespoons confectioners' sugar

1 teaspoon vanilla extract

CUSTARD

1 (11-ounce) package shortbread cookies

1 (8-ounce) package cream cheese, softened

1 (14-ounce) can sweetened condensed milk

1 (5- or 6-ounce) box vanilla pudding

2 cups heavy whipping cream

Fresh berries, for topping

Directions

For the whipping cream, mix heavy cream, confectioners' sugar, and vanilla in a bowl, then beat until medium peaks form.

For the custard, crush the cookies and lay in the bottom of a 9-by-13-inch pan.

Mix the cream cheese and sweetened condensed milk. Set aside.

Make the vanilla pudding using the package directions. Gently fold into the whipping cream.

Gently fold together the cream cheese/condensed milk mixture with the pudding and whipping cream.

Pour over the cookies and refrigerate 4 hours to overnight.

Decorate the top with your favorite fresh berries, and enjoy!

PREP TIME
20 minutes

CHILL TIME
1 hour

SET TIME
1 hour

YIELD
1 (8-by-8-inch) pan

Prayer Fudge

I pray while I cook; I pray while I bake. **I really love the quiet and peace that comes with cooking.** This is one of those recipes I was talking about in the section introduction, the kind that will make your kids and grandchildren say, "Ohhhh, my grammy makes the very best fudge!" Tuck this recipe away and pull it out at Christmastime. It's sure to be loved for generations. My family asks for it now, and each time I make it, I pray over their lives and hearts. Get to praying over your family's future and then eat some damn good fudge. Your family will know you prayed for them while you made it.

Ingredients

1½ cups mini marshmallows
(to fold in at the end)
2 cups granulated sugar
1 cup heavy whipping cream
2½ cups large marshmallows
2 cups semisweet chocolate chips
3 tablespoons butter
1 teaspoon vanilla extract
1 pinch flaky sea salt (optional)
1 cup lightly toasted walnuts

Directions

Chill the mini marshmallows in the refrigerator for 1 hour.

Pour the sugar and cream into a saucepan, then bring to a simmer over medium heat until the sugar is completely dissolved.

Add the large marshmallows. Stir with a wooden spoon, then bring to a low boil over medium to medium-low heat, 5 to 7 minutes. Make sure to stir along the pan's bottom.

Turn the heat off and add the chocolate, butter, vanilla, and salt. Stir to completely melt the butter and chocolate.

Fold in the chilled mini marshmallows and toasted walnuts.

Butter an 8-by-8-inch glass baking pan or line a pan with parchment or nonstick foil. Pour in the fudge and allow to set for 1 hour. Enjoy!

PREP TIME
20 minutes

BAKE TIME
35–40 minutes

YIELD
1 (9-by-9-inch) pan

Walnut Frosties

When I was a little girl, my mom's best friend, Barb, would pick me up to take me on special outings: clothes shopping, thrifting, lunch, a drive up to the mountain. It felt special every time. I'd stay at Barb's house overnight on some of these occasions. I would walk through the door to the smell of deeply caramelized brown sugar and coffee. And there'd be these huge trays of walnut frosties; think pecan pie meets a cookie bar. Thin icing with a gooey, delicious center. **Oh my gosh, they were heavenly**! Here is my take. Tender, buttery crust and delicious icing covering that delicate, nutty brown sugar filling. Enjoy!

Ingredients

CRUST

1¾ cups all-purpose flour

1 cup butter, softened

½ cup granulated sugar

1 pinch salt

FILLING

10 ounces or 2 cups chopped
    walnuts (small dice)

1 cup packed dark brown sugar

2 eggs

½ cup granulated sugar

½ cup mapley syrup

½ cup melted butter

1 teaspoon vanilla extract

1 pinch kosher salt

CREAM CHEESE ICING

4 ounces cream cheese, softened

1½ cups confectioners' sugar

1 teaspoon vanilla extract

1 pinch salt

Directions

Preheat oven to 350°F. Line a baking pan with parchment paper.

For the crust, mix ingredients in a mixing bowl and press the crust into the prepared baking pan, at least 1 inch up the sides of the pan. Bake for 15 minutes.

For the filling, in a mixing bowl, combine the ingredients and pour into the prepared crust.

Bake 35 to 40 minutes. Remove from oven (you should see a slight wobble in the filling) and cool completely before frosting.

For the icing, mix the ingredients in a bowl until smooth, then frost the bars with the icing.

Serve and enjoy!

PREP TIME
15 minutes

CHILL TIME
4 hours to overnight

YIELD
1 (9-by-13-inch) pan

No-Bake Blackberry Cheesecake Slab

Ingredients

1 (11-ounce) package shortbread cookies, such as sandies

½ cup melted butter

4 pints or 4 heaping cups fresh blackberries

3 (8-ounce) packages cream cheese, softened

1 cup sugar

1 tablespoon lemon juice

2 cups heavy whipping cream

Fresh blackberries and mint, for garnish

Directions

Crush the cookies by hand in a gallon ziplock bag (or in a food processor) to a fine crumb. Add the butter and mix well.

Press the crumbs into a glass 9-by-13-inch baking dish and set aside.

Smash the blackberries and press them through a wire mesh strainer or flour mill to remove the seeds. Set the pulp aside and discard the seeds.

In the bowl of your stand mixer (or with a hand mixer), mix the cream cheese and sugar well. Add the blackberry pulp and lemon juice. Mix well. Add the heavy cream and mix until it begins to thicken. The mixture should be thick enough that it doesn't slide easily off a spoon.

Pour the mixture into the prepared crust and refrigerate at least 4 hours or overnight. Overnight yields the best set.

Garnish the top with blackberries and fresh mint leaves.

Serve and enjoy.

PREP TIME
15 minutes

BAKE TIME
12–18 minutes

YIELD
9–12 shortcakes (biscuits)

FRUIT MACERATION TIME
30 minutes

Peach and Berry Shortcakes

Ingredients

BISCUIT DOUGH

3½ cups all-purpose flour

½ cup granulated sugar

1 tablespoon baking powder

1 pinch kosher salt

1½ cups cool butter (not ice cold, but cooler than room temperature)

1–1½ cups heavy cream

Raw sugar for the tops

FRUIT FILLING

4 peaches

2–3 cups fresh strawberries

2 pints fresh raspberries

¼ cup sugar

Juice of a lemon

WHIPPED CREAM

1 (8-ounce) package cream cheese, softened

3 cups heavy whipping cream

½–1 cup confectioners' sugar, depending on desired sweetness

1 tablespoon vanilla extract

1 pinch salt

Directions

Position the oven rack in the center of the oven and preheat oven to 400°F. Line a baking sheet with parchment paper.

I use a stand mixer, but this can easily be done by hand. In a large bowl, combine the flour, granulated sugar, baking powder, and salt, and mix well.

Dice the butter and add to the mixer. If mixing by hand, cut the butter with a pastry cutter or fork into the flour mixture. Mix on low until the butter is cut well throughout the flour. It will look sandy and hold together when pinched between your fingers. The purpose of the cool butter is to create layers as in a traditional biscuit, but the soft butter absorbs into the flour and gives a crumbly shortbread texture to the edges.

Stream the cream into the mix, mixing until it clumps around the paddle, 1 to 2 minutes. Start with 1 cup and add a bit more if needed. You are looking for a shaggy but moist biscuit dough.

Break the dough by hand into craggy balls the shape of a small lemon, roughly ¼ to ⅓ cup apiece.

Sprinkle with raw sugar.

Place on the prepared baking sheet about 2 inches apart. Bake 12 to 18 minutes until slightly puffed and golden.

For the fruit filling, slice the peaches and place in a large mixing bowl. Add the berries, sugar, and lemon juice. Gently fold to mix. Set aside. Let stand at least 30 minutes before serving.

For the whipped cream, add the soft cream cheese to the bowl of a

stand mixer and slowly add the heavy whipping cream. If you do this gradually, you'll avoid lumps.

Add the confectioners' sugar, vanilla, and salt, then mix to combine. Whip until thick and fluffy peaks form.

To assemble, split the shortcakes and fill them with fruit and cream. Serve and enjoy.

*   *Fancy way to let the fruit sugar and lemon juice stand.*

PREP TIME
20 minutes

BAKE TIME
35 minutes

YIELD
1 (9-by-13-inch) pan

Cherry Pie Bars

It's been seven years and counting; **tradition is a very beautiful thing**. These bars aren't actually pie at all. This recipe makes a lovely, buttery pound cake intertwined with cherry pie filling. After many years of making this and calibrating it to fit my family's taste, I've come up with a glorious version I take to absolutely every Fourth of July celebration.

Ingredients

2 cups sugar

1 cup butter, softened

4 eggs

2 cups all-purpose flour

1 teaspoon baking powder

½ teaspoon salt

1 (21-ounce) can cherry pie filling

Directions

Preheat oven to 350°F. Line a 9-by-13-inch pan with parchment paper.

In a stand mixer, or with a hand mixer, cream sugar and butter on low. Add the eggs one at a time. Beat until just combined.

Add the flour, baking powder, and salt. Spread a little over half the cake batter into the pan. Evenly spread the pie filling over top, and spoon the rest of the cake batter over the pie filling. It's fine if the cherries show through.

Bake 35 minutes or until the top has turned slightly golden. Do not overbake. Allow to cool and slice into squares. Enjoy!

PREP TIME
15 minutes

BAKE TIME
30–35 minutes

YIELD
1 (9-by-13-inch) baking pan*

Gooey Lemon Cake Bars

Ingredients

CAKE

2 cups sugar

1 cup butter, softened

4 large or extra-large eggs
(5 if smaller)

1 teaspoon vanilla extract

Zest and juice of 1 lemon

1 pinch kosher salt

2 cups all-purpose flour

1 teaspoon baking powder

CREAM CHEESE FILLING

10 ounces cream cheese,
softened

1 cup sugar

1 egg

⅓ cup fresh-squeezed lemon juice
and zest (1–2 lemons plus zest)

Directions

Preheat oven to 350°F. Line a 9-by-13-inch pan with parchment paper. In a mixing bowl, or in the bowl of your stand mixer, combine the sugar and butter. Mix until combined.

Add the eggs one at a time, mixing between each addition.

Add the vanilla, lemon juice plus zest, and salt. Mix.

Add the flour and baking powder, then mix until just combined.

Spread ⅔ of the cake batter evenly into the prepared pan, and set aside.

For the cream cheese filling, in a separate bowl, with a handheld or stand mixer, mix the soft cream cheese, sugar, egg, and lemon juice and zest until smooth. Pour this cream cheese mixture evenly over the cake batter.

Spoon the remaining ⅓ batter over the top of the cream cheese in dollops. Using a butter knife, spread the dollops out and connect them in long strands. You will not have enough to cover it entirely. You want long strands of batter and cream cheese peeking through.

Bake 30 to 35 minutes. Slightly underdone cake is better than overdone, so pull the cake from the oven when it has a tiny bit of wobble.

Cool and enjoy.

Metal is used for this recipe; may take a bit longer to properly cook in a glass pan.

PREP TIME
20 minutes

BAKE TIME
20–25 minutes

YIELD
1 (9-by-9-inch) pan

Classic Crackle-Top Brownies

Ingredients

½ cup melted butter

½ cup neutral oil suitable for baking (I use olive.)

2 cups sugar

1 teaspoon vanilla extract

½ teaspoon kosher salt

4 eggs

1 cup melted bittersweet chocolate

1 cup all-purpose flour

½ cup unsweetened cocoa powder

10 ounces chopped milk chocolate

Directions

Preheat oven to 350°F. Line a 9-by-9-inch pan with parchment paper.

In a large mixing bowl, whisk the melted butter and oil together. Add the sugar and mix, then add the vanilla and salt. Mix in the eggs. Add the melted chocolate and just barely mix it in, then add the flour and cocoa powder. Stir just until the flour and cocoa have disappeared into the mix, then add chopped chocolate.

Pour the batter into the prepared pan. Bake 20 to 25 minutes; there should be a bit of a wobble in the center when it's ready.

Slice and enjoy.

PREP TIME
15 minutes

BAKE TIME
30–32 minutes

YIELD
1 (9- or 10-inch) skillet

Skillet S'mores Brownie

Ingredients

CRUST

12 full-sized graham crackers

4 tablespoons melted butter (plus more to butter skillet)

1 tablespoon granulated sugar

1 pinch salt

BROWNIES

4 eggs

1 cup dark brown sugar

1 cup granulated sugar

½ cup melted butter

2 tablespoons neutral oil (I use olive)

1 teaspoon vanilla extract

½ teaspoon kosher salt

1 cup all-purpose flour

⅔ cup cocoa powder

3 cups mini marshmallows

Vanilla ice cream, for serving (optional)

Directions

Preheat oven to 350°F. Liberally butter a cast iron skillet.

For the crust, in a bowl or large freezer bag, crush the graham crackers into tiny crumbs. Add the melted butter, sugar, and salt. Mix well and press into the prepared skillet.

For the brownies, whisk the eggs, sugars, butter, oil, vanilla, and salt in a mixing bowl. Gently fold the flour and cocoa powder into the batter. It's okay if it's a bit lumpy; do not overmix.

Pour the brownie batter over the graham cracker crust and bake 20 minutes.

Add the marshmallows to the top and continue to bake another 10 to 12 minutes. There should be a slight wobble in the center of the brownies.

Cool 30 minutes before serving. These brownies are gooey! Spoon and serve with vanilla ice cream for an extra special treat!

PREP TIME
15 minutes

BAKE TIME
35–45 minutes

YIELD
1 (9-by-13-inch) oval

Nutty Oatmeal and Pear Crisp

My mom would make apple crisp often. She'd chop up apples and make an oat topping quickly, and before you knew it, into the oven it went. This is my take on that childhood staple.

Ingredients

FILLING

4–6 cored, diced pears (4–6 cups)

½ cup packed dark brown sugar

½ cup chopped pecans

1 tablespoon cornstarch

1 teaspoon pumpkin pie spice

1 cup apple juice or water

1 tablespoon lemon juice

1 pinch salt

BROWN SUGAR OAT CRUMBLE

½ cup butter, plus 3–4 tablespoons
   (reserved)

¾ cup rolled oats, quick or
   traditional

½ cup packed dark brown sugar

¼ cup all-purpose flour

1 teaspoon vanilla extract

1 pinch salt

TOFFEE SAUCE

1 cup dark brown sugar

1 cup heavy cream

2 tablespoons butter

1 pinch salt

Vanilla ice cream, for serving
   (optional)

Directions

Preheat oven to 350°F. Add the diced pears to your baking dish.

Sprinkle the pears with the sugar, pecans, cornstarch, and pumpkin pie spice. Mix well, then add the apple juice or water, lemon juice, and salt.

For the crumble, in a mixing bowl, smash the butter into the oats, flour, sugar, vanilla, and salt until you have a nice crumble.

Add the crumble to the pears, and dot the top with the reserved butter.

Bake 35 to 45 minutes.

While it bakes, make the toffee sauce. Heat the sugar, cream, and butter in a medium saucepan until the sugar dissolves, then add the salt and stir.

When ready to serve, add vanilla ice cream (optional) to the top of the crisp and drizzle with the toffee sauce.

PREP TIME
15 minutes

BAKE TIME
45 minutes

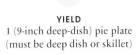

YIELD
1 (9-inch deep-dish) pie plate
(must be deep dish or skillet)

Sour Cream Drop Biscuit and Strawberry Cobbler

Ingredients

COBBLER

4–5 cups fresh strawberries, roughly chopped or quartered

½ cup sugar (more if you like it sweeter)

2 tablespoons cornstarch

1 tablespoon lemon juice

1 pinch salt

BISCUIT TOPPING DOUGH

2 cups all-purpose flour

½ cup sugar

¾ cup cold butter, cubed

1 tablespoon baking powder

¼ teaspoon kosher salt

1 cup half-and-half or buttermilk

Directions

Preheat oven to 375°F. Add the chopped berries to a large mixing bowl.

Top with the sugar, cornstarch, lemon juice, and salt. Mix gently until the sugar and cornstarch melt into the berries.

In a separate large mixing bowl, prepare the biscuit dough. Add the flour, sugar, baking powder, butter, and salt, and mix using a pastry blender, fork, or by pulsing in the work bowl of a food processor. Work the dough until it forms large, crumbly clumps like sand.

Pour in the half-and-half or buttermilk and gently mix.

Butter the pie plate or skillet, then add the berry mixture. Drop the biscuits by the spoonful over the top of the fruit. Bake for 45 to 50 minutes or until the fruit is bubbly and the biscuit top is light golden brown.

Serve with vanilla ice cream or a drizzle of cold heavy whipping cream.

PREP TIME
15 minutes

BAKE TIME
25–35 minutes

YIELD
1 (9-inch deep-dish) pie
plate or skillet

Peach and Cornmeal Shortbread Crumble

This one goes out to my dad. He's a peach man through and through. A couple years ago he'd been asking me to make him a peach cobbler, and for some reason I just hadn't been able to get around to it. My parents live on a lovely lake, and one day my dad slipped and fell in. He found himself trapped under the water, unable to make his way from beneath the low dock. When he recalls the story today, he admits to feeling "like that was it." He thought he was a goner. A part of his clothing had gotten stuck on something, but he eventually managed to free himself and get above the water.

I'll never forget that day. When I heard about his accident, I happened to have peaches on hand, so I fixed up this cobbler and cried when I delivered it to him. He was delighted. He said, "Hey, maybe I'll slip off the dock more often!" We have dark humor in our bones.

As heavy as some of the elements of this story are, it's a lighthearted one. We've all got just a certain amount of time here on this big ol' Earth, and **we've gotta make the most of it**. We've gotta make the pies, fix the cobblers, and bring 'em over when they are specially requested. We just don't know how many breaths we've got. So if there is anything you are putting off doing, by all means, do it. Don't sweat the small stuff, as they say. Enjoy today. As for me, I'll never sit on a special request for a delicious sweet again.

Ingredients

PEACH OR APRICOT FILLING

2 tablespoons butter (for the
   bottom of the skillet or pan)
4–5 cups fresh peaches or
   apricots, skin on or skin off
½–¾ cup sugar; start with ½ cup
   and add more if needed
1 tablespoon cornstarch
1 tablespoon lemon juice

Directions

Preheat oven to 350°F.

Rub the skillet or pie plate with 2 tablespoons of butter. Slice the peaches and place them in the deep-dish pie plate or skillet.

Add the sugar, cornstarch, and lemon juice. Mix well.

For the crust, mix the ingredients in a bowl and pour over the top of the fruit.

CORNMEAL CRUST

1 cup all-purpose flour

¾ cup butter, softened

½ cup cornmeal

½ cup sugar

1 pinch salt

Ice cream, heavy cream, or
    crème fraiche, for serving

Bake 25 to 35 minutes.

Serve with ice cream, heavy cream, or crème fraiche.

A hint at the last of summer...

...when the blueberries arrive.

PREP TIME
15 minutes

BAKE TIME
45–55 minutes

YIELD
1 (9-by-13-inch) pan

Blueberry Buckle

A hint at the last of summer, when the blueberries arrive. The roaring summer lingers on during the month of August. Long days, hot sun, and a carefree lifestyle as long as the berries hang on. Blueberries are summer's final berry to ripen, and they always serve as a bittersweet reminder to me that, with them, the fresh and bright growing season is just weeks away from its close.

All is not lost with the blueberry's arrival, however. The summer still gives glorious produce such as tomatoes and corn clear into September here in the Pacific Northwest. Our relatively moderate climate yields a treasure trove of goodness longer than in other areas of the country.

I say, brave the ovens for a shortbread buckle! A baking session after the heat of the day, with the windows open until 11:00 p.m., is exactly what this recipe is made for. It's also a wonderful way to use frozen blueberries if you are lucky enough to squirrel some away for a summer treat in the middle of a gloomy January Saturday, when you're **craving some warm summertime**. So, make sure you head out and pick blueberries this August! And make sure to tuck some away for winter.

Ingredients

BERRY FILLING
6-8 cups ripe, clean blueberries
½–1 cup sugar, depending on the
     sweetness of your fruit
¼ cup cornstarch
Juice of 1 lemon
1 pinch salt

CRUST
1¾ cups all-purpose flour
1 cup butter, softened
½ cup sugar
1 pinch salt
¾ cup buttermilk

CREAM DRIZZLE
2 cups heavy cream

Directions

Preheat oven to 350°F. In a 9-by-13-inch pan, place the blueberries, sugar, cornstarch, lemon juice, and salt. Mix thoroughly.

For the crust, either in the work bowl of your food processor/stand mixer, with a hand mixer, or by hand, pulse/mix the flour, butter, sugar, and salt until large crumbles form.

Fold the buttermilk into the crumbles.

Evenly spread over the blueberry mixture and bake 45 to 55 minutes, until the fruit filling is bubbling and the crust is golden brown.

Serve warm with cold heavy cream drizzled over top.

PREP TIME
15 minutes

BAKE TIME
35–40 minutes

YIELD
1 (9-by-13-inch) pan

Pineapple and Cherry Dump Cake

We ate dump cakes all the time growing up! They are so easy: a box of yellow cake mix, ⅓ cup of melted butter, and any canned pie filling you can find. We always made pineapple and cherry dump cakes, and my brothers, sister, and I loved them! This little gem is all about the homemade crust and fresh pineapple if you've got it! If not, no worries—canned works fabulously.

Ingredients

4 cups diced pineapple (fresh or
   canned)

2 (24-ounce) cans cherry pie filling

CRUMBLE

1¾ cups all-purpose flour

1 cup plus 4 tablespoons butter,
   softened

¾ cup sugar

½ teaspoon kosher salt

Directions

Preheat oven to 350°F. Butter a 9-by-13-inch baking dish and add the pineapple and cherry pie filling to the bottom.

For the crumble, mix the ingredients (1 cup butter only; reserve the 4 tablespoons) in the bowl of a stand mixer (or use a hand mixer) until soft and crumbly.

Place the crumble evenly over the fruit, and dot with the remaining butter.

Bake 35 to 45 minutes until bubbly and lightly golden on top.

Serve and enjoy.

PREP TIME
30 minutes

CHILL TIME
3–4 hours or overnight

BAKE TIME
40–50 minutes

YIELD
1 (9-by-13-inch) pan

Cranberry Bread Pudding with Cream Cheese Glaze

Ingredients

BREAD PUDDING

3 cups heavy cream

3 eggs

1 cup fresh or frozen cranberries (use dried if you can't find fresh or frozen)

1 cup dark brown sugar

1 cup milk

3–4 tablespoons cubed butter

2 teaspoons vanilla extract

1 teaspoon cinnamon

1 teaspoon kosher salt

5–6 cups cubed chewy artisan bread

TO FINISH

2–3 tablespoons raw sugar

CREAM CHEESE GLAZE

1 (8-ounce) package cream cheese, softened

½ cup granulated sugar

2 tablespoons butter

1 cup heavy whipping cream

1 teaspoon vanilla extract

1 pinch salt

Directions

Place all the bread pudding ingredients except the bread cubes in a large mixing bowl and mix well, making sure to whisk the eggs fully into the cream and sugar. The butter will not incorporate, and that's okay. Next, fold in the bread.

Generously butter a 9-by-13-inch pan and pour the bread pudding mixture into it.

Cover with plastic wrap and refrigerate 3 to 4 hours or overnight.

Preheat oven to 350°F. When it's time to bake, sprinkle the raw sugar on top of the mixture and let stand on the counter 10–15 minutes to take the chill off the dish.

Bake 40 to 50 minutes.

While the bread pudding bakes, make the glaze. Melt the soft cream cheese, sugar, and butter in a medium saucepan over medium heat. Gradually add the cream so it incorporates evenly. A whisk helps. Do not boil.

Once it's melted and mixed, turn off the heat. Then add the vanilla and salt.

To serve, remove the bread pudding from the oven and let cool 20 minutes. Spoon the cream cheese glaze over the top, then serve.

PREP TIME
10 minutes

BAKE TIME
20–22 minutes

YIELD
9–12 large muffins

Giant Mini Chocolate Chip Muffins

Ingredients

1½ cups granulated sugar

2 eggs

½ cup melted butter, cooled

2 teaspoons vanilla extract

½ teaspoon kosher salt

2¼ cups all-purpose flour

1 tablespoon baking powder

2 cups mini chocolate chips

1 cup buttermilk *

Sparkling or raw sugar for the tops

Directions

Preheat oven to 375°F. Line a jumbo muffin tin with paper liners. In a large bowl, combine the sugar, eggs, butter, vanilla, and salt.

Add the flour and baking powder, and gently mix.

Sprinkle in the mini chocolate chips.

Add the buttermilk.

Gently mix, then scoop into the prepared muffin tin. Fill each muffin cup ¾ of the way full, roughly ⅓ of a cup.

Sprinkle with sparkling or raw sugar (This gives the top that signature bakery-style texture and flavor.)

Bake 15 minutes, then decrease the oven temperature to 350° to finish baking, another 5 to 7 minutes.

* *Quick buttermilk alternative: 2 tablespoons of lemon juice plus half-and-half, equaling 1 cup total.*

Pies and
Galettes

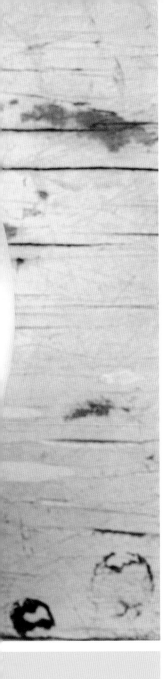

LET'S TALK ABOUT PIE!

Do you prefer a firmer, set fruit filling in your pie? Or a slightly saucier pie filling? For me, I'm team saucy. I love a cornstarch thickener. It provides a glossy fruit filling with a little give. Pie purists will swear by a tapioca thickener, which provides a firmer filling with very little run when you slice it. That's picture perfect, but we aren't living for a photo, friends; we are livin' for saucy scoops mingling with sweet cream ice cream.

And crusts! Let's talk crusts! Are you team Crisco or lard in your piecrusts? I'm gonna make a shocking statement: I'm team all butter all the time. Give me a butter pastry over a shortening pastry *every time*. I'll take that savory sweetness butter adds over the flat taste that shortening provides. I'd be open to a mix of lard and butter, but save all the shortening and Crisco. You might say that shortening provides flakier layers, but I think butter does the job just as well with more flavor.

Come on a short trip to France with me right now in your mind's eye. We are strolling Parisian boulevards, stopping in bakeries and cafés. We order croissants and eclairs, and we get lost in this perfect world of gruyere and pâte brisée. You won't find a tub of shortening in any French bakery. The dream-exceeding, shatteringly crisp layers and tender middles inside of a croissant almondine are made with butter, lamination, and love.

In my cooking, I find inspiration in French and Italian cuisine more than any other. I love ease and eating seasonally. I love French peasant or family food: long braises, simple cheese plates, and green salads dressed with just shallots and vinegar. This stunning, almost magical, thing happens when you opt for a free-form galette instead of a perfectly manicured crust. The edges almost have a shortbread texture, and tiny pools of butter bubble at the edges when it's removed from the oven.

For me, pies are comforting expressions of tradition and, ultimately, love. Pies are steeped in Americana and tradition, butter and beauty, and *nothing artificial*. I concede that your grandmother's recipe may contain shortening, and it's a taste you love! By all means, keep those memories, but make your own memories in butter crusts. I add a touch of sugar and lots of salt to my butter pastry. It yields a crust that's flaky as well as salty.

And we don't just stop at butter pastry! This chapter of the book houses delightful recipes for cream pies, crumb crust pies, and no-bake

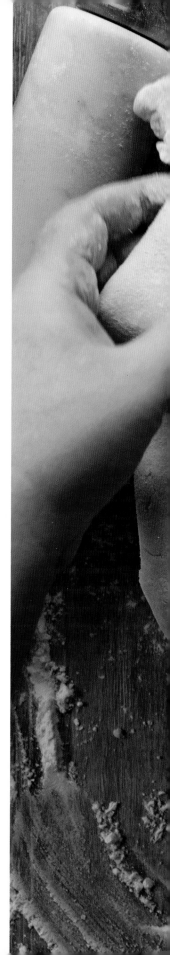

> "For me, pies are comforting
> expressions of tradition and,
> ultimately, love. Pies are steeped in
> Americana and tradition,
> butter and beauty."

cheesecake pies. I think a fruit pie is a delicious expression and the perfect dessert. You've got everything you need for a smile. When you mention fruit pie to me, I'm a little girl again, watching my great-grandmother Thora sprinkle flour across our dining room table with a bowl of apples beside her. It's not glamorous. It's not perfect, and yet it is. I remember her at ninety, her fingers bent the way fingers are after a lifetime of feeding people and living. I remember ripples of butter in the dough. Yes, I'm sure she used Crisco, but that's ruining the memory a bit, so let's just say—yes!—it was butter. It couldn't be anything but butter.

You might say I'm smitten with these recipes, pure and simple. I hope you become smitten too. I hope you find something in here that becomes your family's favorite and that the memories you make to surround that recipe bring you joy. Who knew a little butter and flour could provide so much joy? It just does, and I don't mind one bit.

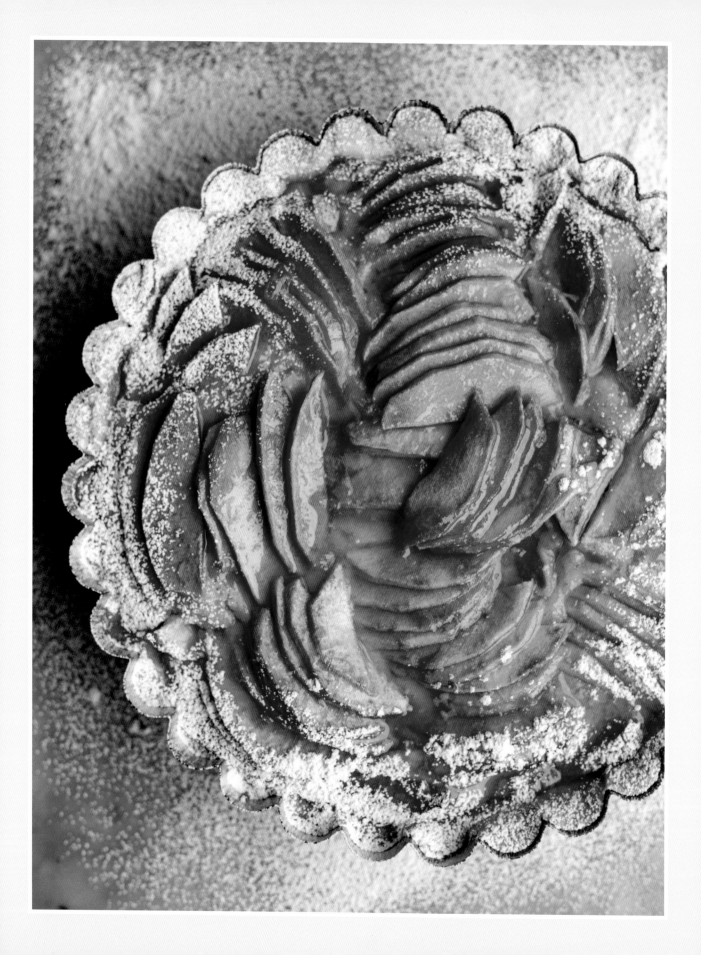

PREP TIME
20 minutes

BAKE TIME
45–55 minutes

YIELD
1 (9-inch) fluted tart pan
with removable sides

French Apple Tart

Ingredients

CRUST

1¾ cups all-purpose flour

1 cup butter, softened

¼ cup sugar

1 pinch salt

FRANGIPANE (ALMOND CREAM)

1¼ cups almond flour (do not use
    superfine almond flour)

1 egg

½ cup sugar

¼ cup plus 2 tablespoons heavy
    cream

¼ cup all-purpose flour

1 teaspoon vanilla extract

1 pinch kosher salt

APPLE FANS

3 pink-flesh apples OR any tart
    apple such as a Pink Lady or
    Granny Smith

2–3 tablespoons sugar

4 tablespoons butter

APRICOT FINISHING GLAZE

½ cup apricot preserves

3 tablespoons hot water

2 tablespoons lemon juice

Directions

Preheat oven to 350°F. In a large mixing bowl, mix the crust ingredients until crumbly and well combined. Press firmly into a 9-inch fluted tart pan with removeable sides, pressing up the sides at least 2 inches.

For the frangipane, in a mixing bowl, combine the ingredients until well combined, then pour directly into the prepared crust.

For the apple fans, slice the "cheeks" off the apples as closely to the core as possible without including the core. You'll get 2 flat halves and 2 smaller sides. Discard the squared core. Thinly slice each cheek.

"Fan" the apple cheeks, keeping each cheek together if possible in a fan shape, and lay each fan gently on top of the frangipane. Cover the entire surface with the apple fans.

Sprinkle the top with sugar and dot with butter. Bake 45 to 55 minutes.

Once the tart is baked, remove from the oven and allow to cool slightly.

For the glaze, in a small bowl, whisk the apricot preserves, water, and lemon juice. Spoon the mixture over the top of the tart. Cool completely before serving.

PREP TIME
1 hour

CHILL TIME
2 hours

YIELD
1 (9-inch deep-dish) pie plate

Black Bottom Banoffee Pie

This one is a British dream. I've been to Europe but never Britain. Though after watching *The Crown*, I think it's safe to say I have an extensive understanding of British culture. Also, I love fish 'n' chips, and western Washington does have a climate like that of England. But I digress. All kidding aside, this little treat is banana and toffee flavored! Thick, luscious dulce de leche, sliced bananas, and (my favorite part) a sneaky ganache layer. I add ganache under the caramel layer, and **it is fabulous**!

Ingredients

CRUST

1 cup cold cubed butter

2½ cups flour

¼ cup granulated sugar

Pinch of salt

Ice water

DULCE DE LECHE

1 (14-ounce) can sweetened
    condensed milk

8 ounces soft cream cheese

2 tablespoons butter

Pinch of salt

GANACHE

½ cup whipping cream

1 cup chocolate chips

2 ripe bananas sliced

Directions

In a mixing bowl or the work bowl of your stand mixer, work the cold butter into the flour, sugar, and salt. Stream in just enough cold water, roughly ¼ cup, to make a shaggy dough. Dump the crust out onto a lightly floured surface and divide into 2 equal parts. Wrap in plastic wrap, flatten, and refrigerate 30 minutes.

Preheat the oven to 350°F. Once the crust is chilled, on a floured surface, roll out a circle of dough 3 to 4 inches larger than your pie plate. Gently transfer the rolled-out crust to the pie plate, cover with a sheet of parchment paper, then add 1 pound of dry beans as pie weights.

Bake the weighted crust 15 to 20 minutes, remove the beans, then bake another 10 to 15 minutes until the crust is golden brown. Remove the crust from the oven and cool completely.

For the dulce de leche, bring the condensed milk to a simmer over medium heat. Cook until it turns a deep golden color, maybe 7 to 8 minutes. It should be the consistency of peanut butter. Add the cream cheese, butter, and salt. Mix until well combined. Set aside to cool.

Next, begin the ganache. Melt the cream and chocolate over low heat, or in 30-second bursts in the microwave.

For the whipped cream, in a large bowl, whip the ingredients together. Divide in two.

WHIPPED CREAM

2 cups heavy cream

¼ cup confectioners' sugar

Pinch of salt

Vanilla

TOPPER

1 ounce dark chocolate, grated

In a large mixing bowl, add the cooled dulce de leche cream cheese mixture to half the whipped cream, then mix completely.

To assemble the pie, pour your cooled but not cold ganache into the bottom of the cooled pie shell.

Arrange the bananas on top of the ganache, then top with the dulce de leche caramel whip.

Finish by topping with the reserved whipped cream and shaved chocolate. Refrigerate for 4 hours or overnight. I think overnight is best.

PREP TIME
1 hour

BAKE TIME
25 minutes

CHILL TIME
4 hours to overnight

YIELD
1 (9-inch deep-dish) pie plate

Silky Coconut Cream Pie

Ingredients

COCONUT CUSTARD

2½ cups heavy cream

4 egg yolks

¾ cup granulated sugar

½ cup whole milk

¼ cup cornstarch

1 pinch salt

2 tablespoons butter

1–2 teaspoons pure coconut
   extract

1 teaspoon vanilla extract

1 cup sweetened shredded
   coconut

PASTRY

2½ cups flour

¼ cup granulated sugar

1 pinch salt

1 cup cold, cubed butter

Ice water

Directions

For the custard, place the heavy cream, egg yolks, sugar, whole milk, cornstarch, and salt in a medium-sized pot and whisk over medium heat. Simmer but do not boil, until the pudding thickens, roughly 7 to 10 minutes. Whisk continually so you don't scramble the egg yolks. The pudding should be thick but never curdled.

Once the pudding is thickened, remove from heat and continue whisking. Add the butter and extracts. Stir until the butter has melted.

Pour through a fine mesh sieve into a mixing bowl and set aside. Add the sweetened shredded coconut. Mix.

Allow to stand 15 to 20 minutes, then put the whole bowl into the fridge to chill.

For the pastry, in a mixing bowl, or the work bowl of your stand mixer, combine the flour, sugar, and salt, then work the cold butter into the mixture. Stream in enough ice water to make a shaggy dough, roughly ¼ cup. Dump the dough onto a lightly floured surface and divide into 2 equal parts. Wrap both in plastic wrap and flatten, then refrigerate 30 minutes. The second disc may be used for another pie or frozen.

Preheat oven to 350°. Once the crust is chilled, on a floured surface, roll out a circle 3 to 4 inches larger than your pie plate.

Gently transfer the rolled crust to the pie plate. Tuck and pinch the crust to fit the plate. Prick the dough's bottom all over with a fork. Place a sheet of parchment paper over the top and add 1 pound of dry beans as pie weights.

WHIPPED CREAM TOPPING

2 cups heavy whipping cream

2–3 tablespoons confectioners'
  sugar

TOPPING

½ cup large toasted coconut
  flakes

Bake the weighted crust 15 to 20 minutes, then remove the weights and bake another 10 to 15 minutes until the crust is golden brown. Remove the crust and cool completely.

To assemble the pie, whip the heavy cream and confectioners' sugar to semi-stiff peaks. Fold 1 cup of the whipping cream into the pudding and pour the mixture into the cooled pie shell.

Top with the remaining whipped cream and the large toasted coconut flakes. Refrigerate at least 4 hours. Overnight is best! Enjoy!

PREP TIME
15 minutes

CHILL TIME
4 hours to overnight

YIELD
1 (9-inch oval or round deep-dish) pie

Deep-Dish Peanut Butter Pie

Ingredients

1 (3.4-ounce) box instant vanilla
  pudding

2 cups heavy cream

1 cup milk

1 cup crunchy peanut butter (use
  smooth if preferred)

1 teaspoon vanilla extract

1 pinch salt

10–12 Biscoff cookies, graham
  crackers, or crunchy peanut
  butter cookies

4 tablespoons butter, melted

1½ cups heavy whipping cream

3 tablespoons confectioners' sugar

Directions

Whip the pudding mix with the cream and milk in a large mixing bowl, then add the peanut butter, vanilla, and salt. Continue mixing until it's light and thick, roughly 2 to 3 minutes.

Crush the cookies in a bowl or ziplock bag and mix with the melted butter.

Press into the pie dish, then spoon the filling into the dish.

Whip the heavy whipping cream in the work bowl of your stand mixer, with a hand mixer, or by hand in a mixing bowl and confectioners' sugar. Top the filling with the whipped cream.

Refrigerate at least 4 hours, but overnight is best!

Serve and enjoy.

PREP TIME
30 minutes

CHILL TIME
30 minutes

BAKE TIME
45–60 minutes

YIELD
1 (10-inch) tart

Rhubarb and Frangipane Galette

Ingredients

PASTRY

½ cup plus 3 tablespoons cold
   salted butter cubes

1½ cups all-purpose flour

1 tablespoon sugar

1 pinch kosher salt

3 tablespoons ice water

FRANGIPANE

1¼ cups almond flour (do not use
   fine or superfine almond flour)

1 egg

½ cup heavy cream

½ cup sugar

¼ cup all-purpose flour

1 teaspoon vanilla extract

1 pinch kosher salt

RHUBARB FILLING

4 cups sliced rhubarb

1 cup sugar

¼ cup all-purpose flour

Splash of water (to make sure there
   are no dry bits of sugar and flour
   on the bottom of the bowl)

2 tablespoons butter

Directions

For the pastry, work the cold butter into the flour, sugar, and salt with a fork, your hands, a pastry cutter, or a stand mixer. I use a stand mixer.

Stream the ice water into the mix until it just comes together. Dump the pastry onto a lightly floured surface.

Press into a round disk that is roughly 1-inch thick. Wrap in plastic wrap and allow to rest in the fridge 30 minutes or up to 3 days.

Once the pastry has finished its rest, bring it out of the fridge. Preheat oven to 350°F. For the frangipane, in a bowl, combine all the ingredients. Mix until it becomes a thick paste. Set aside.

For the rhubarb filling, in another bowl, combine the ingredients and mix thoroughly.

To assemble your tart, roll out the pastry on a floured surface into a circle roughly 12 inches across. Transfer the pastry to the tart pan and press into the pan, taking care to press up the sides. Spread the frangipane onto the crust and pour the rhubarb over the top. Dot the top with butter and bake 45 to 60 minutes.

Serve and enjoy.

PREP TIME
20 minutes

CHILL TIME
20–30 minutes

BAKE TIME
45–60 minutes

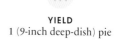
YIELD
1 (9-inch deep-dish) pie

Chocolate and Bourbon Pecan Pie

Pecan pie is an iconic American dessert that shows up at just about every Thanksgiving and Christmas gathering! It's my husband's all-time favorite pie, and I've aimed to create a twist on this classic that will make this recipe famous among your loved ones! Bourbon, dark chocolate, and that buttery caramel filling can't be beat! Here is **a winner**, in *every* sense of the word. I hope you try this version and that your family absolutely loves it!

Ingredients

BUTTER PASTRY CRUST

1 cup cold butter

2 cups all-purpose flour

¼ cup ice water

1 pinch kosher salt

FILLING

1 cup packed dark brown sugar

½ cup granulated sugar

3 eggs

½ cup melted butter

½ cup dark corn syrup

⅛ cup bourbon

1 teaspoon vanilla extract

10 ounces pecans

1 pinch kosher salt

¼ cup semisweet chocolate chips

Directions

For the pastry crust, in the bowl of your stand mixer or with a hand mixer (or by hand using a pastry cutter), mix the cold butter and salt into the flour until it forms into small balls, each about the size of a raisin. Add ice water and mix the dough until just comes together. Press the crust into a disk and wrap in plastic wrap, then refrigerate 20 to 30 minutes. Remove the crust from the fridge and allow it to stand 5 minutes before rolling out into a 12- to 13-inch circle on a floured surface.

Meanwhile, preheat oven to 350°F. For the filling, in a large mixing bowl, mix the sugars, eggs, butter, corn syrup, bourbon, and vanilla. Once you've got a smooth batter, fold in the pecans and kosher salt. Set aside.

Press the rolled pastry crust into your deep-dish pie plate. Trim the excess and leave a ½-inch overhang around the rim of the pie dish. Tuck that ½-inch under and crimp the edge however you prefer. Pour the chocolate chips into the bottom of the crust. Pour the filling over the top and bake 45 to 60 minutes. If the pie browns too quickly, place foil over top. Enjoy!

Note:
A great silky caramel pecan pie will always have a slight wobble in the center. As the pie cools, the wobble will set. If there is no wobble, the pie is overcooked and the eggs may curdle a bit but still taste lovely.

PREP TIME
10 minutes

CHILL TIME
4 hours to overnight

YIELD
1 (9-inch) pie

No-Bake Malted Hazelnut Chocolate Cream Pie

Ingredients

CRUST

18 Oreos

3 tablespoons melted butter

FILLING

1 (8-ounce) package cream cheese, softened

1 heaping cup Nutella

2 cups heavy whipping cream

¼ cup confectioners' sugar

2 heaping tablespoons unsweetened cocoa powder

1 tablespoon malted milk powder

2 teaspoons vanilla extract

1–2 teaspoons hazelnut liqueur, often known as Frangelico (optional) (Start with 1 teaspoon and add more depending on how strong you like it.)

1 teaspoon hazelnut extract (Sometimes difficult to find. Skip it if you can't find it.)

1 pinch salt

TOPPING

2 cups heavy whipping cream

½ cup confectioners' sugar

1 tablespoon malted milk powder

1 pinch salt

½ cup toasted hazelnuts, chopped

Directions

For the crust, crush the Oreo cookies in a large ziplock bag and place into a large bowl, then add the melted butter. Press the buttered crumbs into the base of a pie plate. At this point you can bake the crust in a preheated 350°F oven for 10 minutes, but it's optional.

For the filling, in a large mixing bowl, with a hand mixer, whip the cream cheese with the Nutella, scrape down the sides of the mixing bowl, then whip again. Once the mixture is smooth with no lumps, add the whipping cream, confectioners' sugar, cocoa powder, milk powder, vanilla, hazelnut liqueur, hazelnut extract, and salt. Continue to whip until thick and creamy.

Pour the filling into the prepared crust and refrigerate for at least 4 hours.

Once you are ready to serve the pie, whip the topping. Add the whipping cream, confectioners' sugar, milk powder, and salt to a mixing bowl, or use the work bowl of your stand mixer, and whip to soft peaks.

Top the chilled pie, and sprinkle with chopped toasted or candied hazelnuts.* Enjoy!

* *To make candied hazelnuts, bring 1 cup sugar to a boil with 2 to 3 tablespoons of water until it becomes a deep brown color but is not burned. You are taking the sugar to the hard crack stage. Add 1¼ cups toasted hazelnuts and a pinch of salt, then stir to combine and pour out onto a parchment-lined baking sheet. I like to form small clusters. Do not touch these until they are completely cooled, then you can break them apart if you need. They will have a crunch to them. Use on top of sweets and yogurt bowls.*

PREP TIME
25–30 minutes

BAKE TIME
35 minutes (total)

CHILL TIME
4 hours to overnight

YIELD
1 (9-inch) tart

Toasted Marshmallow Lemon Meringue Pie

Even the name sounds a bit intimidating. There are several classic techniques for making meringue, all yielding delicious marshmallow-like clouds to adorn your favorite custards, curds, and cream pies. I've experimented with different methods (once even shattering a glass double boiler!). Much to my surprise, I found that when enough sugar is involved in whipping egg whites, the whites—which we've always been warned to handle with delicacy—are pretty darn stable, as in that air really isn't going anywhere. It's a thing of beauty!

When I create a recipe with shortcuts, I must first master the original and uncover the flaws. If a recipe is great or standard, why? Are there any places I can improve the process, taste, and experience? In a world where everyone has a recipe for everything, I make sure I've made a **better, different, simple take on a classic**.

Enter my lemon meringue! I wanted a custard that was far from the diner gel many people think of, and honestly, I didn't want to make a separate curd that might need to be pushed through a mesh sieve. I like to mix and pour and bake. Several recipes were too eggy. Though this basically a lemon-egg pie, I don't want to taste any egg while I'm eating. Then I remembered my good friend sweetened condensed milk. A classic key lime pie is simply made of eggs, condensed milk, and key lime juice. I'm in love with that texture! So I baked a butter shortbread-like crust, followed key lime pie's lead, and **a star was born**. I cut out further steps and topped it with billows of stable meringue. I think we could all use more stability in our lives.

This meringue is like an old friend. I can't be bothered with piping or fussing. I need simple, rustic swoops and plops! I don't fancy the taste of butane, so I skip the blow torch and allow this pie a trip under the broiler! It's best chilled the next morning, served out of a mug, with a cup of hot coffee for breakfast.

Ingredients

CRUST

1¼ cups all-purpose flour

¾ cup (1 stick plus 4 tablespoons)
   soft salted butter

½ cup almond flour

1 tablespoon sugar

1 pinch kosher salt

Directions

Preheat oven to 350°F. For the crust, mix the all-purpose flour, butter, almond flour, sugar, and salt in the work bowl of your stand mixer, with a hand mixer, or by hand, until it's crumbly like damp sand. Press the crust firmly into your pie or tart pan, working it evenly up the sides. Bake 25 minutes or until the crust is lightly golden.

FILLING

1 (14-ounce) can sweetened
    condensed milk

4 large or extra-large egg yolks

Juice of 3 lemons

Juice of 1 lime (use an extra
    lemon if you don't have a lime)

1 tablespoon lemon zest

1 pinch kosher salt

MERINGUE TOPPING

4 large or extra-large egg whites

¾ cup sugar

1 pinch kosher salt

For the filling, mix all the ingredients until well combined. If the crust has puffed up or shrunk, you can use the bottom of glass or a measuring cup to gently press the crust back into shape and up the sides of the pan. Pour the filling into the baked tart or pie shell. Return to the oven and bake 12 to 14 minutes. The center will be jiggly. Cool to room temperature before refrigerating.

Meanwhile, for the meringue, whip the egg whites, sugar, and salt in the work bowl of your stand mixer or with your hand mixer until you have glossy, stiff (but not overly stiff) peaks. This takes about 7 to 9 minutes. Swirl the fluffy meringue over the top of the pie and place under a broiler for 1 to 2 minutes to gently brown the top. It takes toasting the meringue further to get that toasty marshmallow effect. Refrigerate at least 4 hours before serving; overnight is best. Enjoy!

Tips:

The meringue may weep or drip sugar syrup in the oven if it is humid in your kitchen or raining outside. This is absolutely fine! Continue to bake it, and it will dry up a bit. This can be a sign of overmixing, undermixing, or humidity. My meringue dropped a touch as it was a very rainy day, but it served just fine.

This can be made a day in advance; just store each element separately and wait to assemble prior to serving.

PREP TIME
30 minutes

BAKE TIME
60 minutes

YIELD
4–6 servings

Pavlova with Lemon Curd and Cream

Ingredients

PAVLOVA

5 egg whites

1 cup granulated sugar

¾ cup confectioners' sugar

1 heaping tablespoon cornstarch

1 pinch salt

1 teaspoon vanilla extract

½ teaspoon white vinegar

LEMON CURD

½ cup butter

1½ cups granulated sugar

1 pinch salt

5 egg yolks

1 whole egg

Juice of 3 lemons

Directions

Preheat oven to 275°F. For the pavlova, in the bowl of your stand mixer or with a hand mixer, beat the egg whites until frothy.

In another mixing bowl, whisk together the sugars, cornstarch, and salt. Add the sugar mixture to the egg whites bowl a quarter cup at a time. Continue to beat and add sugar until you've reached a glossy medium peak where the meringue holds its shape. No sugar granules should be felt when pressing the mixture between your thumb and forefinger. Add the vanilla and vinegar, then beat to combine.

Line a baking sheet with parchment paper. Spoon the meringue into the center of the sheet and make sure it has peaks and swirls. It should be roughly 3 inches tall and 8 to 9 inches across. Bake 60 minutes. Crack the oven door open and turn the oven off, allowing the pavlova to cool completely inside the cooling oven.

For the lemon curd, melt the butter in a saucepan and whisk in the sugar and salt. Quickly whisk the egg yolks and the whole egg into the mixture. Add the lemon juice and heat gently over medium-low heat until the mixture thickens, about 10 minutes. This will cook more quickly on a gas stove, so be aware of your heat and timing. Increase the heat to medium if cooking on an electric stovetop. Press the mixture through a metal sieve to remove any lumps or bits of cooked egg. Allow to cool completely.

SOFT WHIPPED CREAM

2 cups heavy whipping cream

½ cup confectioners' sugar

1 pinch salt

1 teaspoon vanilla extract

2 cups sliced fresh strawberries, for
   topping

Lemon zest, for garnish

For the whipped cream, beat the cream, sugar, and salt in a large mixing
bowl with a hand mixer until soft, pillowy peaks appear. Mix in the
vanilla.

To assemble the pavlova, place the meringue onto a serving dish, top
with lemon curd and whipped cream, and then top that with sliced
strawberries. Add lemon zest for a garnish.

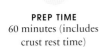
PREP TIME
60 minutes (includes crust rest time)

CHILL TIME
30 minutes

BAKE TIME
50–60 minutes

SET TIME
2–4 hours

YIELD
1 (9-inch deep-dish) pie

Silky Smooth Cream Cheese Pumpkin Pie

Don't think "cheesecake" when you see this recipe, think "impossibly smooth, creamy, traditional pumpkin pie." In a blind taste test, you probably wouldn't know there was even cream cheese in it. I've been after a "best ever" pumpkin pie recipe for years. This year I thought I'd try my hand at a salted caramel pumpkin pie…but it was too sweet, and I didn't want this salty bite. Then, after trying sour cream and mascarpone, I decided that cream cheese was exactly where I wanted to be. It has the right amount of heft and tangy cream-cheesiness to potentially create the **pumpkin pie of my dreams**.

I was right! And it feels good! This will officially be the only pumpkin pie you ever make from now on. It's marvelous and traditional and oh so wonderful. Happy Thanksgiving, friends. This year, love on your family and be grateful for the days that—even with their hardships—offer us brilliant lessons and, sometimes, good pie.

Ingredients

CRUST

2 cups all-purpose flour

1 cup cold butter, cubed

2 tablespoons granulated sugar

1 pinch salt

¼ cup ice water

Directions

First, prepare the crust. In the work bowl of your stand mixer, with a hand mixer, or by hand, combine the flour, butter, sugar, and salt, then mix until the dough has the consistency of gravel.

Add the ice water and mix until it forms a shaggy dough.

Form the shaggy dough into a disk. Place the disk into a plastic bag or wrap in plastic wrap, then refrigerate for at least 30 minutes. This dough freezes great or keeps 3 days in the fridge before rolling.

When you are ready to make the pie, remove the dough from the fridge and leave on the countertop for 4 to 5 minutes.

Then roll out the dough onto a floured surface and make a roughly 14- to 16-inch circle. Lay it in the deep-dish pie plate. If using a shallow pie plate, you will have enough for two crusts.

Trim the excess and crimp the edges however you choose.

FILLING

- 1 (8-ounce) package cream cheese, softened
- 3 eggs, room temperature
- 1¼ cups packed dark brown sugar
- 1¼ cups evaporated milk
- 1 (15-ounce) can pumpkin purée, or 2½ cups fresh roasted pumpkin
- 1 tablespoon vanilla extract
- 1 teaspoon cinnamon
- ½ teaspoon pumpkin pie spice
- 1 pinch salt

For the filling, in a large mixing bowl, combine the soft cream cheese with the eggs, one at a time, mixing until smooth and creamy with no lumps.

Add the sugar and evaporated milk. Mix.

Add the remaining ingredients, then mix until completely combined.

Pour the filling into prepared deep-dish pie plate with crust. Bake 55 to 60 minutes.

The pie will have a wobbly center when it's finished. Allow to set 2 to 4 hours before slicing. The wobble will completely set as the pie cools. Enjoy!

PREP TIME
20 minutes

CHILL TIME
4+ hours

BAKE TIME
30 minutes

YIELD
1 (9-inch) fluted tart

Creamy Mango Lime Tarts

Hi, summer, it's us! We need something sweet, cool, creamy, and perfect. Yes! We need mango lime curd poured into a buttery crust and topped with fruit and cream. This one will wow your friends. In fact, this tart was born because I wanted to make something dreamy and different for friends who were coming to visit!

I'm a sucker for lemon curd, so I figured I'd give mango a try. The first attempt at this dessert was too sweet and needed a citrus punch. Then I added lime juice. **Pure magic!** I decorated with stone fruit and currants, and it was so pretty. And pretty delicious. Enjoy!

Ingredients

FILLING

1 cup mango purée (2–3 fresh
    mangos, peeled and seeded)
1 cup melted butter
1 cup granulated sugar
3 eggs
½ cup lime juice (juice and zest
    of 3 limes)
1 pinch salt

CRUST

1¾ cups all-purpose flour
1 cup butter, softened
¼ cup granulated sugar
1 pinch salt

WHIPPED CREAM

1 cup whipping cream
2 tablespoons confectioners' sugar
1 teaspoon vanilla extract
1 pinch salt

Directions

For the filling, pour all the ingredients into a medium-sized saucepan and cook over medium heat until thickened, about 7 to 10 minutes. Simmer but do not boil.

Once the mixture thickens, pass it through a fine mesh sieve to remove any eggy bits. Set aside to cool.

Preheat oven to 350°F.

For the crust, mix all the ingredients in a large bowl, then press into a tart pan with removable sides. Press the crust at least 1 inch up the sides of the pan.

Place a sheet of parchment paper over the crust and add 1 pound of dry beans as pie weights.

Bake weighted crust 15 to 20 minutes, then remove the weights and bake another 5 minutes. Allow to cool.

Pour the filling into the cooled crust, then refrigerate 4+ hours. Overnight is best.

For the whipped cream, in a large mixing bowl with a hand mixer, whisk together all the ingredients until you reach medium peaks. Top the tart and enjoy!

TIP:
Feel free to top
with stone fruits
or currants!

PREP TIME
10 minutes

BAKE TIME
35–40 minutes

YIELD
¼ sheet pan

Sugared Plum Tart

Ingredients

2 sheets frozen puff pastry, thawed
    and rolled to fit the pan

10–12 small, black, or Italian plums,
    halved, or 5–7 larger plums,
    sliced (Use what you can find in
    your local grocer.)

¾ cup sugar

2 tablespoons lemon juice

2–3 tablespoons cornstarch

1 teaspoon vanilla bean paste or
    vanilla extract

1 pinch salt

2–3 tablespoons sugar

Directions

Preheat oven to 350°F. Line a baking sheet with parchment paper and fit the pastry into the lined sheet pan. Roll the 2 sheets of pastry out on a floured surface. Overlapping is fine. Fit the pastry sheets into the quarter sheet pan with some pastry hanging over the edge.

Mix the sliced plums with the sugar, lemon juice, cornstarch, vanilla, and salt.

Pour the plum mixture onto the puff pastry and arrange them cut-side up.

Sprinkle the remaining sugar on top. Bake 35 to 45 minutes until the fruit is bubbly and the pastry golden brown. Cool and serve.

PREP TIME
30 minutes

CHILL TIME
4+ hours

YIELD
1 (9-inch deep dish) pie

Raspberry Chantilly Cream Pie

Ingredients

FILLING

1 (8-ounce) package cream
    cheese, softened
2 pints fresh raspberries, divided
1 envelope gelatin
⅓ cup apple juice
2 tablespoons lemon juice
1 tablespoon raspberry liqueur
1 teaspoon pure raspberry
    flavoring or extract (optional)
2 cups heavy whipping cream
1–2 cups confectioners' sugar
    (depending on how sweet
    you prefer it)

SHORTBREAD CRUST

15–18 shortbread cookies
5 tablespoons melted butter

Directions

In a large mixing bowl or in the bowl of your stand mixer, whisk the softened cream cheese into 1 pint of the raspberries until completely smooth.

In a small bowl, bloom the gelatin in the apple and lemon juice, liqueur, and extract for 3 to 4 minutes. It'll start to thicken. Continually stir with a whisk to break up lumps.

Add the bloomed gelatin to the filling mixture and whisk on medium speed until fully incorporated.

Add the heavy cream, scraping the sides, and mix until smooth and creamy.

Add the confectioners' sugar, 1 cup at a time, tasting for sweetness. The sweetness of your berries makes a big difference in the amount of sugar you'll add. Mix completely. Continue to whip until it becomes light and fluffy but does not separate. It should reach the texture of thick whipped cream.

For the crust, preheat oven to 350°F. Whirl the cookies and melted butter in a food processor until you've got a crumb that resembles wet sand.

Press the crumbs into a pie plate and bake 15 minutes. Allow to cool.

Pour the finished filling into the cooled crust and decorate the top of the pie with the remaining fresh raspberries. Refrigerate at least 4 hours, but I find overnight is best. If you taste any grit from the gelatin, it needs more chill time in the fridge.

PREP TIME
10 minutes

COOK TIME
20 minutes

CHILL TIME
4 hours to overnight

BAKE TIME
10 minutes

YIELD
1 (9-inch) pie

Whiskey S'mores Pie

Ingredients

CHOCOLATE CUSTARD FILLING

1 cup sugar

½ cup unsweetened cocoa
   powder

¼ cup cornstarch

2 ounces dark chocolate

1 pinch salt

3 egg yolks

2 cups milk

1 cup heavy cream

2 tablespoons butter

3 tablespoons whiskey of choice*

1 teaspoon vanilla extract

GRAHAM CRUST

11 graham crackers

6 tablespoons melted butter

1 tablespoon sugar

1 pinch salt

MARSHMALLOW MERINGUE TOP

3 egg whites

1 pinch salt

1 cup sugar

Directions

For the custard filling, in a saucepan over medium heat, combine the sugar, cocoa powder, cornstarch, dark chocolate, and salt.

In a mixing bowl, whisk the egg yolks into the milk and cream, then slowly stream this mixture into the chocolate mixture.

Whisk continually until it thickens but does not boil, 5 to 6 minutes. Turn off heat and set aside.

Add the butter, whiskey, and vanilla, then stir until glossy and well combined.

For the crust, pulse all ingredients in a food processor, then press into your 9-inch pie plate. Bake 10 minutes at 350°F. Cool slightly and set aside.

Finally, when ready to serve, you'll make the marshmallow meringue top. Combine the egg whites and salt in the work bowl of your stand mixer (or use a hand mixer) and beat on medium-high speed 7 to 8 minutes. Gradually add the sugar, mixing until glossy stiff peaks form and the granulated sugar can no longer be felt between your fingers when touched.

To assemble the pie, pour the hot custard into the warm crust, and chill at least 4 hours or overnight before adding the meringue top. When ready to serve, make the meringue and top the chilled pie. Use a torch or broiler to toast the edges. Serve immediately. This pie keeps well up to 3 days in the refrigerator.

* *To keep this nonalcoholic, just eliminate the whiskey. It's delicious either way!*

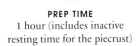
PREP TIME
1 hour (includes inactive
resting time for the piecrust)

CHILL TIME
30 minutes

BAKE TIME
45–60 minutes

YIELD
1 (9-inch deep-dish) pie

Not Your Granny's All-Butter, Double-Crust-Pastry Fruit Pie

Sometimes you need a pie recipe that is easily modifiable. You want a good ol' standby method that's as flexible as you are! Take whatever fruit you have on hand, make a double pastry crust, and you are set! The sky is the limit.

This method works well with pears and cranberries. If we're talking pie filling, plums or cherries are fantastic too. This all-butter double pastry crust works with every fruit imaginable. For this book, I wanted to use **fruits that would represent each season**. It's a choose-your-own-adventure pie for sure—you can use strawberry and rhubarb, blueberry, peach, or apple.

When I was growing up, my granny Thora didn't use cornstarch; she used flour to thicken fruit pies. This method isn't wrong, but if you want a clear, thick syrup, I find that cornstarch gives that glossy fruit pie center. I've made the switch, but when I'm out of cornstarch, I use flour in a pinch.

Ingredients

STRAWBERRY RHUBARB FILLING

2½–3 cups diced fresh strawberries
(Amount depends on the size
of your fruit; you want a full fruit
filling.)

2 cups diced fresh rhubarb

½–¾ cup granulated sugar
(depending on how sweet your
fruit is)

2 tablespoons butter

1 teaspoon cornstarch

1 pinch salt

Directions

Mix the ingredients for the filling you've chosen in a mixing bowl and set aside.

For the crust, in a mixing bowl or the work bowl of your stand mixer, work the cold butter into the flour, sugar, and salt. Stream in ice water to make a shaggy dough, roughly ¼ cup.

Dump the dough onto a lightly floured surface and divide into 2 equal parts. Wrap each in plastic wrap and flatten. Refrigerate 30 minutes.

Preheat oven to 350°F. Once the dough is chilled, on a floured surface, roll out a circle 3 to 4 inches larger than your pie plate.

Gently transfer the rolled crust to the pie plate and fill with your filling of choice.

PEACH OR APRICOT FILLING

5 cups fresh fruit, skin on or off
   according to preference
½–¾ cup granulated sugar
1 tablespoon lemon juice
1 teaspoon cornstarch

APPLE FILLING

4 tart baking apples like Granny
   Smith or Pink Lady
½–¾ cup dark brown sugar
1 teaspoon cornstarch
1 teaspoon cinnamon
1 teaspoon apple pie spice or
   pumpkin pie spice
1 pinch salt

BLUEBERRY FILLING

5 cups fresh or frozen blueberries
½–¾ cup granulated sugar
1–2 tablespoons lemon juice
1 teaspoon cornstarch

DOUBLE-CRUST PASTRY

1 cup cold, cubed butter
2½ cups all-purpose flour
¼ cup granulated sugar
1 pinch salt
Ice water (I use just under ¼ cup)

EGG WASH

1 beaten egg

Large sparkling sugar or raw sugar,
   for garnish (optional)

Roll the second crust 1 inch larger than the diameter of your pie plate.

Lay the crust over the filled pie and press the two crusts' edges together. Fold any excess under into the lip of the pie plate. Press and pinch the edge to decorate.

Press a sharp knife into the center to vent the pie. In a small bowl, combine the beaten egg and ¼ cup water. Brush the pie in egg wash and sprinkle with raw sugar (optional).

Place on a baking sheet and bake 45 to 60 minutes, or until the crust is golden brown and the fruit is bubbling.

Allow to cool for at least 15 minutes before serving.

Cakes

FIRED AND CAKE

I spent five years of my life being hired and fired from banks. I started working at the local army base's bank when I was nineteen, and I was a teller. We balanced our tills using a paper ledger and then transferred the numbers into a computer. Well, my till rarely balanced. They moved me around to different departments, and I struggled to find my place.

I made friends, though. Oh my gosh, did I ever! The women I worked with were all military spouses, and they took me right in. I learned things about different cultures and faraway places. Each day in the lunchroom we'd talk politics, religion, motherhood, and marriage. No one was ever offended; no one was ever cross. Each woman held completely different views of the world from the one beside her. No one owned a cell phone, and there was no social media. There were just these stories in the break room at lunch, and the shifts rotated.

I got to taste real Korean food and true southern grits. I had "pee-can" sticky buns and rice rolls with seaweed and avocado. I was the youngest of the bunch. I tasted "real chocolate," according to my Scottish boss, and a lamington from an Australian coworker.

I have many memories from that workplace, not all centered on food. I stood with one of these lovely women and cried on 9/11. I chatted with every customer, some of whose faces I can still recall in vivid detail. I had crushes on lots of the cute soldiers.

As I said, my till was always off: $20 over, $10 short. It never balanced. I worked there almost a year. One day my sweet Scottish boss called me back to her office. I knew what was coming. She held a box of tissues and said, "These are for me." I was puzzled at first, but she pulled out a tissue and tears filled her eyes. "I'm so sorry, Danielle, but I have to let you go. I've never in my life fired someone who I think is such a wonderful person. You are a gem of a human. My heart aches. I'm not sure banking is for you, but I am sure you'll be just fine."

I stood up and gave her a hug. I understood. I did struggle, but I really loved the job despite that. I walked to my car defeated, yet my heart was full. I'd miss those ladies. Though banking ultimately wasn't for me, I did spend the next five years employed at two other banks. I found the culture was the same: loving, forgiving, and nurturing. I was no good at banking, but I was good with people. I loved chatting with my coworkers, and I

"I'm twenty-one years away from my bank days, but I think about those women often. Sure, a lot of the names have faded, but the way those women made me feel, along with the foods they brought in from their kitchens, stand vibrantly in my memory."

loved the way these women embraced each other although they came from so many walks of life and shared so many different opinions about the workings of the world.

One standout recipe from my time at the bank was an upside-down German chocolate cake. Eating it, I'm reminded of this special period during my young adulthood when it seemed possible to love each other devoid of any "me first" mentality. It makes me think about sisterhood and strong, diverse ladies just doing life together. It's truly a cake to bridge barriers.

I'm twenty-one years away from my bank days, but I think about those women often. Sure, a lot of the names have faded, but the way those women made me feel, along with the foods they brought in from their kitchens, stand vibrantly in my memory. It seems fitting to bring people together over cake. It's no coincidence we bring cakes to parties, serve baked and frosted showstoppers at weddings, and choose our favorite cakes to celebrate birthdays.

This chapter is full of beautiful cakes and beautiful memories. Bake one or four and make beautiful memories of your own.

A star was born.

PREP TIME
15 minutes

BAKE TIME
40–50 minutes

YIELD
1 standard loaf

Nutella Banana Cake

I reserve the right to say I invented this version of banana bread! About eight years ago we were on a big Nutella kick, and I try to make at least two to three loaves of banana bread per month for my kiddos. I added Nutella to my loaf prebake, and **a star was born**. I posted it to the internet. It went viral. This was back in the days when you would post a recipe and forsake any hope that you'd receive credit. But I know I started an online wave; this recipe began showing up all over the web. I know it's not traceable, but I'll carry the honor with me all my days. Give it a go—it's wildly delicious!

Ingredients

3 overly ripe bananas

1½ cups packed dark brown sugar

2 eggs

1 tablespoon vanilla extract

1 teaspoon kosher salt

½ teaspoon cinnamon

½ cup melted butter

¼ cup olive oil

2 cups all-purpose flour

2 teaspoons baking powder

½ teaspoon baking soda

¼ cup sour cream

½ cup Nutella plus 2 tablespoons
   for the top, once cooled

Directions

Preheat oven to 350°F. Line a loaf pan with parchment paper and butter. In a large mixing bowl, smash the bananas with a fork and add the dark brown sugar, eggs, vanilla, salt, and cinnamon.

Add the melted butter and olive oil, then mix.

Add the flour, baking powder, and baking soda. Mix. While there are still ribbons of flour in the mixture, add the sour cream. Mix to incorporate, but don't overmix.

Pour the batter into the prepared loaf pan.

Add the Nutella in an even line down the center of the batter.

Using a butter knife, gently swirl 2 to 3 times, making a pretty Nutella pattern on top. Bake 40 to 50 minutes.

Once the bread is done baking and cooled, add two tablespoons of Nutella on top.

The Nutella may cause a dip in the bread. This is not a sunken loaf; it's the weight of the hazelnut spread. It's delicious and perfect!

Serve and enjoy!

PREP TIME
30 minutes

BAKE TIME
45–50 minutes

CHILL TIME
(for the lemon curd)
1–2 hours

YIELD
1 standard angel food cake

A Simpler Way to Angel Food

I picked up an old aluminum angel food cake pan at the thrift store, and it sat in my garage for nearly all the pandemic. My four-year-old, Milo, pulled it out a few weeks ago and made it his favorite toy. I hadn't even cleaned it. I mean, it had been washed, but in the deep crevasses there were still bits of cake stuck from the previous owner.

For a moment I romanticized where the pan came from, who celebrated with this pan and made glorious, soft angel food cakes topped with cream and fruit. Today, I searched the house for the pan. I haven't had angel food cake in nearly twenty years. Growing up, it was the cake of choice for baby showers, bridal showers, and—always for me—birthdays. We ate angel food cake all the time. One year, my mom's best friend adopted children from Bulgaria, and at those precious babies' welcome party, I remember sitting in the corner of a big, beautiful home eating a slice of angel food cake with blueberry and strawberry sauce.

I've been thinking much lately about living in the moment, **not taking a bit of time for granted**. That's hard to do! There can be so much on our plates as mothers and wives. But I turned forty this year, and I have a new, beautiful appreciation for life. When the sun's out, I'm grateful. When the seasons change, I anticipate it with childlike excitement. I'm more aware of the seasons and how fast time goes now, and I savor daffodil season giving way to tulips and then to peonies.

When I looked at that angel food cake pan with remnants of old celebrations still in it and thought about the woman who baked with it, I remembered my own beautiful angel food memories and felt inspired to try my hand at making one for my kids. I read at least a dozen recipes and took the best tips from each, simplifying to come up with foolproof angel food cake.

I'll never know whose pan I picked up at the thrift store, but I'd like to believe it was a woman who loved life, her family, and celebrating with fluffy, delicate cake. I am grateful to have bought her old cake pan. It'll bring joy to my boys for years to come. **May you breathe in all life has to offer in this moment and have a slice of cake**.

Ingredients

EGG WHITE MIXTURE

12 (roughly 1½ cups) room-
   temperature egg whites

1 round teaspoon cream of tartar

1 teaspoon vanilla extract

½ teaspoon kosher salt

½ cup granulated sugar

FLOUR MIXTURE

1 shy cup all-purpose flour (*shy
   meaning barely full*)

1 cup granulated sugar

½ tablespoon cornstarch

GARNISH OPTIONS

Whipped cream

Fresh berries

Lemon curd

Directions

Preheat oven to 350°F.

In the work bowl of your stand mixer, add the egg whites, cream of tartar, vanilla, and salt. Beat on medium speed until foamy peaks appear.

Gradually add the sugar. Adding it all at once stops the whites from staying fluffy.

While the egg whites beat, add the flour, sugar, and cornstarch to a separate mixing bowl. Whisk 2 minutes.

Once the egg whites have been beaten to stiff peaks, add ⅓ of the sugar–flour mixture and gently fold it into the whites. Do not overmix.

Pour into an ungreased angel food cake pan.

Bake 45 to 50 minutes. DO NOT open the oven door. Remove the cake from the oven when it's golden brown and puffed up completely. Immediately invert it onto the counter or onto a bottle to allow it to cool completely.

Serve and enjoy!

6-YOLK LEMON CURD TOPPING

6 egg yolks

2 cups sugar

¾ cup fresh lemon juice (juice of 4–5 lemons)

½ cup butter

Heat a saucepan over medium heat.

Place all ingredients in the saucepan.

Whisk continually while the mixture melts.

Whisk until the mixture is 180°F and begins to thicken and steam. Do not boil or simmer.

Pass through a mesh strainer to remove any lumps.

Chill the curd for 1 to 2 hours before serving. It's lovely warm so if you can't help yourself…enjoy!

Serve the angel food cake with lemon curd, whipped cream, and fresh berries! Enjoy!

PREP TIME
15 minutes

BAKE TIME
30–35 minutes

YIELD
2 (9-inch) round cake

The Very Best Carrot Cake with Walnuts and Apricot Jam

This is truly the carrot cake to end all carrot cakes. The pièce de résistance is the addition of tangy apricot jam laced with lemon juice, which tops the wildly creamy cream cheese icing. **You're gonna flip when you taste it!** Walnuts, golden raisins, and an ample amount of shredded carrots turn this into the spice cake of one's dreams! Listen to me—if you are a carrot cake fan, try this! It'll become your family's favorite cake, a cake that will be requested for birthdays and celebrations for years to come. My great-aunt Libby had a carrot cake recipe in a book of recipes that was a bit bland and needed love. I've tinkered with this recipe for years, and this is yet again another rendition. I dedicate this variation to Libby, with love. I think she'd approve.

Ingredients

4 eggs

½ cup melted butter

½ cup olive oil

¼ cup plain full-fat Greek yogurt

1 tablespoon vanilla extract

1 teaspoon cinnamon

½ teaspoon kosher salt

1½ cups packed dark brown sugar

½ cup granulated sugar

2 cups all-purpose flour

2 teaspoons baking powder

½ teaspoon baking soda

4 cups shredded carrots (4–5 carrots)

1 cup rough chopped walnuts, not too finely diced, plus additional for topping

1 cup golden raisins

Directions

Preheat oven to 350°F. Grease and flour the 2 (9-inch) cake pans.

In a large mixing bowl, whisk the eggs, melted butter, oil, Greek yogurt, vanilla, cinnamon, and salt together.

Add the sugars and mix.

Add the flour, baking powder, and baking soda. Gently mix. Add the shredded carrots, walnuts, and raisins.

Fold the batter until it's completely mixed, but do not overmix.

Divide the batter evenly into each pan.

Bake 30 to 35 minutes or until the cakes are firm to touch in the center and a pick comes out with moist crumbs on it. Gone are the days of a dry toothpick—that's the indication of an overdone cake. Cool the cakes completely before icing.

For the cream cheese icing, add the ingredients to the work bowl of your stand mixer (you may hand mix as well). Mix until smooth and creamy. The icing may look dry at first, but give it at least 2 minutes.

GARNISH

½ cup chopped walnuts (to garnish the outer rim of the iced cake)

CREAM CHEESE ICING

4 cups confectioners' sugar

1 (8-ounce) package cream cheese, softened

4 tablespoons butter, softened

3 tablespoons heavy cream

1 teaspoon vanilla extract

APRICOT JAM TOPPER

1 cup apricot jam

2 tablespoons lemon juice

It comes together nicely. Add a touch more cream if you like it thinner.

For the jam topper, mix the jam and lemon juice. Set aside.

To frost the cakes, turn one cake out onto a plate. Cover with half the icing. Spread to the edges, then place the other cake on top.

Add the rest of the icing and spread to the edges. I use the back of a spoon to do this.

Add a rim of chopped walnuts to the top outer edge, then pour the thinned jam directly into the center of the cake. Smooth it out with the back of a spoon.

This cake can be enjoyed immediately, but it loves a rest of at least an hour for a cleaner slice.

PREP TIME
15 minutes

BAKE TIME
35–40 minutes

YIELD
1 (9-by-13-inch) pan

Circus Animal Cookie Cake

If any of the recipes here embody the **heart and soul of this book**, it's this cake. This cake is whimsical and lighthearted. Billowy pillows of baby-pink marshmallow frosting and those itty-bitty sprinkles that immediately take you back to childhood, to a tiny dish of iced animal crackers. It took two years and lots of flops to come up with a series of cakes that needed only to have their ingredients placed in a bowl and mixed—no creaming, no adding ingredients in thirds. There is a place and time for more technical recipes, but honestly, in the midst of raising kids, working, and throwing birthday parties, we all need a magical dump-and-stir cake requiring little effort for a big, fat payoff. By the way, I love slicing a 9-by-13-inch cake in half and stacking one half right on top of the other!

Ingredients

2½ cups all-purpose flour

2 cups sugar

1 tablespoon baking powder

½ teaspoon kosher salt

5 egg whites

¾ cup sour cream

½ cup soft melted butter (This is a key step. Your butter won't be completely melted, but it'll be halfway between soft and melted.)

½ cup neutral oil

½ cup milk or buttermilk

1 tablespoon vanilla bean paste or vanilla extract

½ cup rainbow sprinkles (jimmies)

Directions

Preheat oven to 350°F. Butter and flour, or spray, a 9-by-13-inch metal baking pan. (I use Baker's Joy spray.)

Add the flour, sugar, baking powder, and salt to a large mixing bowl or the bowl of your stand mixer. Mix or whisk to combine.

Add the melty butter, egg whites, sour cream, oil, milk or buttermilk, and vanilla. Mix until combined, being careful not to overmix.

Add the rainbow sprinkles and just barely mix.

Pour the batter into the prepared pan.

Bake 35 to 40 minutes; do not overbake. Once the cake is baked, remove from the oven and cool completely.

When the cake is cool, turn it out onto a large platter or board. Slice it directly in half.

For the frosting, add the sugar, egg whites, lemon juice, and cream of tartar to a heavy-bottom pot.* Use a hand mixer to beat the mixture over medium heat for 7 minutes. Make sure you do not mix up the sides of the pot to avoid reintroducing sugar crystals as you beat.

PINK 7-MINUTE FROSTING

2 cups sugar

5 egg whites

1 tablespoon lemon juice

½ teaspoon cream of tartar

1 pinch salt

2 drops red food coloring

1 tablespoon small ball rainbow
　　sprinkles (nonpareils)

During the last moments, add just 2 to 4 drops of red food coloring to
make the frosting pink.

Spread 1½ cups of the frosting on the first half of the sliced cake, then
place the other half of the cake directly on top. This frosting is soft and
may smoosh over the sides. Let it drip; it's just fine. You may also not
need all of the frosting.

Spread the other half of the frosting on top, and use the back of a spoon
to create peaks and valleys. Sprinkle the small ball rainbow sprinkles on
top. Slice and enjoy.

* *If you prefer a double-boiler method, go for it! I find that gentle, even heat*
　works fabulously for me, so I skip the double boiler altogether.

Tip:
Note the frosting takes on a different texture the next day. It's best eaten the day it's made.

PREP TIME
10 minutes

BAKE TIME
35–45 minutes

YIELD
1 standard loaf

Summertime Zucchini Bread

Ingredients

2 cups grated zucchini

1½ cups packed dark brown sugar

2 eggs

½ cup olive oil

⅛ cup molasses

2 teaspoons vanilla extract

1 teaspoon cinnamon

½ teaspoon kosher salt

2 cups all-purpose flour

2 teaspoons baking powder

½ teaspoon baking soda

1 cup chopped walnuts

Directions

Preheat oven to 350°F. Line a loaf pan with parchment paper.

In a mixing bowl, mix the zucchini, brown sugar, eggs, oil, molasses, vanilla, cinnamon, and salt until well combined.

Fold in the flour, baking powder, and baking soda. Mix until it just comes together, then fold in the walnuts. Do not overmix.

Pour the batter into the loaf pan, and bake 35 to 45 minutes or until a pick inserted in the center of the loaf comes out with a touch of crumb on it.

PREP TIME
10 minutes

BAKE TIME
25–30 minutes

YIELD
1 (9-by-9-inch) square cake

Tender Gingerbread Cake

Ingredients

1 cup packed muscovado sugar
  (dark brown works great)

½ cup plus 2 tablespoons butter,
  softened

1 teaspoon vanilla extract

2 eggs, room temperature

¼ cup plain full-fat Greek or plain
  yogurt

1¾ cups all-purpose flour

1 teaspoon baking powder

½ teaspoon kosher salt

½ teaspoon cinnamon

¼ teaspoon ground cloves

¼ teaspoon ground ginger

¼ teaspoon apple pie spice

1 cup hot water

¾ cup molasses

GARNISHES

½ cup confectioners' sugar

1 cup pomegranate arils

Directions

Preheat oven to 350°F. Line a 9-by-9-inch cake pan with parchment paper.

Cream the sugar, butter, and vanilla on low speed 3 minutes. Add the eggs one at a time and mix until just incorporated, then scrape down the sides of the bowl and gently fold the yogurt into the batter.

In a separate bowl, whisk the flour, baking powder, salt, and spices together.

In a third bowl, mix the hot water and molasses together.

Now mix the dry ingredients into the batter in 3 additions, alternating with the hot molasses water. Do not overmix.

Pour the batter into your lined pan and bake 25 to 30 minutes until the cake is well baked. Allow the gingerbread to cool, then dust with confectioners' sugar and pomegranate arils. This cake is also lovely with cream cheese icing!

Serve and enjoy!

PREP TIME
15 minutes

BAKE TIME
24–28 minutes

YIELD
2 (9-inch) cakes

Black Forest Birthday Cake

I'll always remember this as my twenty-fourth birthday cake. **This cake is a remedy** for me when I long for that free-and-easy feeling, that desire to fly away and experience a different way of life. It makes a mighty fine birthday cake as well!

Ingredients

2 cups sugar

1¾ cups all-purpose flour

1 cup melted butter

1 cup cocoa powder

4 eggs

¾ cup plain Greek yogurt

2 teaspoons vanilla extract

1 tablespoon baking powder

½ teaspoon kosher salt

1 cup very hot water or coffee

GLOSSY FUDGE GLAZE

1¼ cups heavy cream

1 cup butter

1 cup sugar

1 cup unsweetened cocoa powder

1 pinch salt

FILLING

1 (24-ounce) can cherry pie filling

1 cup fresh cherries, pitted and
    sliced (optional)

Directions

Preheat oven to 350°F. Butter and flour, or spray, 2 (9-inch) round cake pans. Set aside.

In a large mixing bowl, gently mix all cake ingredients except hot water or coffee.

Once it comes together, add the hot water or coffee, then mix until smooth, making sure to scrape down the sides of the bowl.

Divide the batter evenly between the prepped cake pans. Bake 24 to 28 minutes.

While the cakes bake, prepare the glaze. In a small saucepan over medium heat, heat all fudge glaze ingredients until the sugar is dissolved, roughly 5 to 7 minutes. Cool to room temperature before glazing but no need to refrigerate. If the glaze has not set enough, it will run off the cake, so make sure you've let it stand long enough to firm up so that it has some movement but is not a runny glaze. It should be thick. Use about ½ cup.

To assemble the cake, turn one cake out onto a large plate, spread half the cherry pie filling on the cake, then top with the fudge glaze.

Place the other cake on top and repeat with the cherries and glaze. You may want to let the thick glaze run over the sides. There's no need to use all the glaze, unless that's desired. This cake will slice messy at first, but as it sets, it will slice cleaner. If you desire perfect slices, cool in the fridge overnight before slicing.

PREP TIME
20 minutes

BAKE TIME
50–55 minutes

CRUST BAKE TIME
10 minutes

INACTIVE TIME
2 hours plus chill time

YIELD
1 (9-inch deep-dish) cake

Ricotta Cheesecake with Fresh Fruit

No skimpy cheesecakes allowed! This thick, showstopping beauty is a **dazzler**.

A cheesecake is a must in any dessert book, especially a cheesecake that's foolproof. No water baths, minimal ingredients, and a big payoff. I was reading the table of contents for this book to my sister, Jenny, and she stopped me: "Wait, I didn't hear any cheesecakes!"

I was nervous. I told her, "Look, those are HARD!" She said, "C'mon, you've got this. Start testing and figure out why it's hard, then fix it. You can't have a desert book without at least two cheesecakes."

I agreed. She was right. I happened to have five pounds of ricotta in my fridge (food stylist problems), so I figured that it all came down to this: I needed a ricotta cheesecake in this book as well as a chocolate cheesecake. They were musts. Thank heaven for ricotta. And thank the good Lord for the Italians.

This cheesecake is **chef's-kiss perfect**. Thank you, Jenny! You can use any fruit that's in season. Cherries and peaches with a little lemon juice and sugar work wonderfully here. This cheesecake is light and rich and sure to make your family very happy.

Ingredients

FILLING

5 cups whole milk ricotta, room temperature

1 (8-ounce) package cream cheese, softened

4 eggs, room temperature

2 cups sugar

⅓ cup all-purpose flour

Juice and zest of 1 lemon

1 tablespoon vanilla extract

1 pinch salt

½ cup melted butter

Directions

Preheat oven to 350°F. In a large bowl with a hand mixer (or with a stand mixer), mix the ricotta, softened cream cheese, and eggs together until smooth.

Add the sugar, flour, lemon juice and zest, vanilla, and salt. Mix until creamy and smooth, making sure you scrape down the sides of the bowl, and mix again to ensure there are no lumps.

With the mixer on low, slowly add the melted butter.

For the crust, put the graham crackers in a large freezer bag and pound gently with a rolling pin to make fine crumbs, or process them in your food processor using the pulse option.

CRUST

13 graham crackers

4 tablespoons butter, melted

1 pinch salt

FRUIT TOPPING

½ cup blueberries

3-4 sliced strawberries

1-2 thinly sliced peaches

Juice of 1 lemon

2-3 tablespoons sugar

Fresh lemon thyme or mint, for
   topping

Fresh macerated fruit, for garnish

Add the melted butter and salt to the crumbs. Mix well and press into a springform pan. Work the crumbs 1 inch up the sides of the pan.

Bake 10 minutes. Remove from the oven and spray the exposed inner rim of the springform pan with nonstick baking spray. I use Baker's Joy. The pan will be hot, so it will sizzle. Do not spray on the crumb crust.

Pour the entire filling mixture into the hot crust.

Return to the oven and bake 50 to 55 minutes. Turn the oven off and allow the cheesecake to cool inside the oven. Crack the door open a few times to allow intense heat to escape.

Refrigerate at least 4 hours or overnight. (I always do overnight.)

To prepare the fruit topping, combine the fruit, lemon juice, and sugar. Allow to stand at room temperature 10 minutes for a syrup to develop. Add fresh lemon thyme or mint for a pop of color and herbaceous freshness.

When it's time to serve, slice the cheesecake and garnish with fresh macerated fruit.

PREP TIME
15 minutes

BAKE TIME
28–32 minutes

YIELD
1 (9-by-13-inch) cake

Classic White Cake with Tuxedo Frosting

Ingredients

CAKE

2½ cups all-purpose flour

2 cups granulated sugar

1 tablespoon baking powder

½ teaspoon kosher salt

5 egg whites

¾ cup sour cream

½ cup melted butter

½ cup neutral oil (I use light olive oil.)

½ cup milk or buttermilk

1 tablespoon vanilla bean paste or vanilla extract

TUXEDO FROSTING

1 (8-ounce) package cream cheese

½ cup salted butter, softened

1 teaspoon vanilla extract

1 pinch salt

3-4 cups confectioners' sugar (Start with three, see how you like it, and add more if you like it sweeter.)

2 tablespoons unsweetened cocoa powder

1 tablespoon heavy cream, if needed

Directions

Preheat oven to 350°F. Butter and flour, or spray, a 9-by-13-inch baking pan. Add the flour, sugar, baking powder, and salt to a large mixing bowl or the bowl of your stand mixer. Mix or whisk to combine.

Add the egg whites, sour cream, melted butter, oil, milk or buttermilk, and vanilla, then mix until combined. Do not overmix.

Pour the batter into the prepared cake pan. Bake 28 to 32 minutes.

For the tuxedo frosting, cream the cream cheese, butter, vanilla, and salt. Add the confectioners' sugar. Mix to combine.

Remove half the frosting to a separate bowl and add the cocoa powder to it. Mix to combine, then add the cream if your chocolate frosting feels too thick. Now you have two different frostings, one vanilla and one chocolate.

Frost the cake in the pan or turn the cake out onto a large serving board or platter. Make large dollops of frosting, alternating between chocolate and vanilla. Gently swirl the frostings together using a butter knife. Once you've reached the marble pattern of your dreams, serve and enjoy!

PREP TIME
15 minutes

BAKE TIME
25–30 minutes

YIELD
1 (9-inch) cake, square or round

Gramma Thora's Walnut and Sour Cream Cake

I know that this cake may only be a whisper compared to the boisterous shout of my great-grandmother Thora's cake, but for this book I knew I had to try something that at least approached what she made. She never baked a cake from scratch and preferred a box mix. I do love a box cake mix. And according to her children, there was a walnut-and-date filling that she'd spread on top of the cake as you would a frosting. And then she'd top *that* with an actual sour cream frosting.

I thought a tender snack cake laced with walnuts and a dollop of brown sugar cream served as a lovely tribute and a delightful mashup between two worlds, a legacy from my great-grandmother and the restaurant that started my career. The brown sugar cream recipe is from my old restaurant, Minoela, and it was a menu staple, topping pound cakes and chocolate cakes.

Ingredients

1½ cups granulated sugar

2 eggs

½ cup butter (halfway between melted and solid, not hot)

2 teaspoons vanilla extract

½ teaspoon kosher salt

2 cups all-purpose flour

1 tablespoon baking powder

1 cup buttermilk

1 cup finely diced walnuts

BROWN SUGAR SOUR CREAM

½ cup dark brown sugar

Splash of vanilla extract

1 pinch salt

3 cups sour cream

Directions

Preheat oven to 400°F. Butter and flour your 9-inch cake pan. In a large mixing bowl, combine the sugar, eggs, butter, vanilla, and salt.

Add the flour and baking powder, and gently mix.

Add the walnuts. Gently mix, then add the buttermilk and fold it into the batter. Then scoop the batter into a 9-inch round or square cake pan.

Sprinkle the raw sugar on top of the cake prior to baking.

Bake 15 minutes, then decrease the oven temperature to 350°F to finish baking, another 10 to 15 minutes.

Remove the cake from the oven, and cool before frosting and serving.

While the cake bakes, make the brown sugar sour cream. Gently fold the brown sugar, vanilla, and salt into the sour cream. Do not overmix or mix too fast. The brown sugar should swirl into the sour cream but not yet fully integrate. Refrigerate.

DATE JAM

1½ cups pitted dates

½ cup apple juice

3 tablespoons soft butter

Pinch of salt

Sparkling or raw sugar for the top

Once the sugar ribbons have melted a bit, gently stir to combine the sugar and cream fully. If you rush this process, the sour cream will become thin in texture. By taking your time, you maintain a thick consistency.

For the date jam, bring the dates and juice to a simmer and smash the dates to form a jam-like consistency.

Cool to room temperature, and smash the dates into the butter. Add the pinch of salt and set aside.

To serve the cake, slice and dollop with the jam and the cream. Sprinkle with the raw sugar, if desired.

PREP TIME
20 minutes

BAKE TIME
35–40 minutes

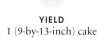

YIELD
1 (9-by-13-inch) cake

Bank Ladies Upside-Down German Chocolate Cake

This is the cake from those banking days I mentioned in the opening of this section. I remember the woman I worked with who gave me the recipe: she had short, naturally blond hair with bangs. She could cook, let me tell you! She was all of forty-five years old, but to a nineteen-year-old me, she seemed so much older. As I'm nearly that age now, I laugh looking back on this.

While working at the bank, we would sometimes have lunchtime potlucks. I got to try many new and unique-to-me foods the women would bring in from home. One woman had a lot of cats, and we'd always find cat hair in the cookies she brought. Some of the other girls on the teller line would joke that she had her cats make the treats. It sounds much less funny on paper yet is hysterical in my mind, imagining a short-haired orange cat stirring up the batter and patting it out into cookies.

This cake is a true gem. It has all the qualities you'd love about a "true" German chocolate cake, but somehow it feels easier. Enjoy!

Ingredients

- 2 cups granulated sugar
- 1¾ cups all-purpose flour
- 1 cup melted butter
- 1 cup cocoa powder
- 1 cup buttermilk
- 4 eggs
- 1 tablespoon baking powder
- 2 teaspoons vanilla extract
- ½ teaspoon kosher salt
- 1 cup boiling hot water or coffee

Directions

Preheat oven to 350°F. Butter, flour, then line a 9-by-13-inch baking pan with parchment paper.

In a large mixing bowl, add the sugar, flour, butter, cocoa powder, buttermilk, eggs, baking powder, vanilla, and salt. Gently mix.

Once it comes together, add the water or coffee, then mix until smooth, making sure to scrape down the sides of the bowl.

Pour the batter into the prepared pan.

For the cream cheese filling, melt the confectioners' sugar, cream cheese, and butter in a saucepan over medium heat. Whisk to smooth out any lumps.

CREAM CHEESE FILLING

3 cups confectioners' sugar

1 (8-ounce) package cream
   cheese, softened

½ cup butter

TOFFEE SAUCE

1 cup dark brown sugar

¾ cup heavy cream

4 tablespoons butter

TOPPINGS

2 cups chopped pecans

2 cups sweetened shredded
   coconut

1 pinch salt

Sprinkle the pecans and coconut evenly over the entire cake.

Pour the melted cream cheese evenly over the cake batter. The cream cheese will sink, but do not worry.

Make the toffee sauce in the same pan. Just melt all ingredients until the sugar is dissolved.

Bake 28 to 35 minutes.

Once the cake is finished baking, allow to cool 10 to 15 minutes, then invert the cake onto a platter. Remove the parchment paper and pour the warm toffee sauce over the top.

Serve and enjoy.

PREP TIME
10 minutes

BAKE TIME
30–38 minutes

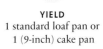

YIELD
1 standard loaf pan or
1 (9-inch) cake pan

Semolina and Almond Cake

If you are looking for something **simple and unfussy** with a wild payoff, then this little cake is it! The semolina flour makes sure the texture stays moist, with a nice crumb. Serve it plain or with fresh whipped cream and strawberries. It's perfect for breakfast, it fits any season, and you really can't mess it up.

Ingredients

- 1 cup sugar
- ½ cup butter, softened
- 1 egg, room temperature
- 1 teaspoon vanilla extract
- ½ teaspoon almond extract
- ½ teaspoon flaky sea salt
- ¼ cup milk
- ¼ cup sour cream
- 1 cup semolina flour
- ½ cup sliced almonds
- ⅓ cup all-purpose flour
- 2 teaspoons baking powder
- 2 tablespoons sliced almonds

Directions

Preheat oven to 350°F. Butter and flour a loaf pan.

In a large mixing bowl, cream together the sugar and butter.

Add the egg, extracts, and salt. Mix.

Add the milk and sour cream, then fold to mix. Add the semolina flour, almonds, all-purpose flour, and baking powder. Mix until it just comes together.

Evenly spread the batter in the prepared pan. Sprinkle the sliced almonds on top. Bake 30 to 38 minutes. This is a moist cake, so if the center is undercooked, it will sink.

Serve and enjoy.

PREP TIME
10 minutes

BAKE TIME
40–55 minutes

YIELD
1 (10-inch) round cake

Buttermilk, Cherry, and Pistachio Cake

Ingredients

1½ cups granulated sugar

¾ cup butter, softened

2 eggs

1¾ cups all-purpose flour

¾ cup cream or half-and-half

2 tablespoons buttermilk powder

1 tablespoon baking powder

1 teaspoon vanilla extract

½ teaspoon kosher salt

1 cup pitted, chopped fresh
    cherries

½ cup chopped pistachios

Confectioners' sugar for dusting

Cold brew coffee and cream with
    a splash of brown sugar syrup,
    for serving

Directions

Preheat oven to 350°F. Line your cake pan with a square of parchment paper, and make sure to leave an overhang in case the cake expands too much during baking. The paper aids in ensuring taller sides.

Cream the sugar and butter until smooth in a large mixing bowl, and add each egg separately, beating after each addition. Add the flour, cream, buttermilk powder, baking powder, vanilla, and salt, and mix until the batter is thick, smooth, and just comes together. Do not overmix. This batter will be very thick.

Spread into your cake pan. Evenly sprinkle the cherries and pistachios over the top of the cake. Bake 45 to 60 minutes. *

Allow the cake to cool, then dust with confectioners' sugar. Slice and enjoy with cold brew coffee and cream, with a splash of brown sugar syrup.

* Because this cake has a high fat content, it will puff up and bake, and then settle flat with a deep golden-brown chewy top. The weight of the cherries will cause them to sink into the cake, and that's okay. It's a moist and delicious cake that's very hard to ruin. Feel free to substitute any fresh chopped fruit and nuts.

Optional:
Serve chilled with fresh orange or mandarin slices.

PREP TIME
10 minutes

BAKE TIME
20–25 minutes

CHILL TIME
1 hour

YIELD
1 (9-inch) cake

Chocolate Orange Flourless Cake

Ingredients

1½ cups dark or bittersweet
    chocolate or chocolate chips

½ cup salted butter

1 cup sugar

1 tablespoon Grand Marnier or
    any orange liqueur

1 teaspoon pure orange extract

1 teaspoon vanilla extract

1 pinch salt

4 eggs

⅓ cup cocoa powder

**DARK CHOCOLATE ORANGE
GANACHE**

½ cup dark chocolate

⅓ cup heavy cream

½ teaspoon orange extract

½ teaspoon Grand Marnier or any
    orange liqueur

Fresh orange or mandarin slices,
    for serving (optional)

Directions

Preheat oven to 350°F. Generously butter and cocoa a 9-inch pie plate or cake pan.

In a medium saucepan, begin melting the chocolate and butter over medium-low heat, but turn the heat off before the chocolate is completely melted. The residual heat will melt the butter and chocolate fully.

In the same saucepan, stir in the sugar, liqueur, extracts, and salt.

Beat the eggs and add them to the mixture, then mix completely.

Gently fold in the cocoa powder.

Pour the batter into the prepared pan and bake 20 to 25 minutes.

Remove from oven, cool slightly, and refrigerate for 1 hour before pouring the ganache over top.

For the ganache, in a saucepan, begin melting the chocolate and heavy cream, but turn the heat off before the chocolate is fully melted. Add the extract and liqueur and stir. Cool slightly.

Pour the ganache over the top of the cake.

PREP TIME
20 minutes

BAKE TIME
30–35 minutes

YIELD
1 (9-by-13-inch) cake

Noah's Apple Cake with a Streusel Top

When my son Noah was in the second grade, they had a week celebrating German food. I was assigned to make the apple cake. His teacher sent home a recipe, which was quite bland, but I was fascinated by how few ingredients the cake had. I made one cake according to the written recipe, which contained only oil, white sugar, apples, and flour. Then I added butter, brown sugar, vanilla, salt, and cinnamon. The result was fantastic!

My kids gobble this cake up when I make it, and it's **tender and flavorful** every time! And give this cake to your babies often. I close my eyes and still see tiny baby hands holding a slice of this cake. Pure gold!

Ingredients

STREUSEL TOPPING

¾ cup all-purpose flour

½ cup very soft butter

½ cup granulated sugar

1 pinch salt

CAKE

3 eggs, room temperature

½ cup melted butter

½ cup vegetable oil (any neutral oil works)

2 cups all-purpose flour

2 cups dark brown sugar

2 teaspoons vanilla extract

1 teaspoon kosher salt

½ teaspoon cinnamon

½ teaspoon baking soda

4 cups peeled, diced apples (I used 4 medium-sized apples: Honeycrisp, Fuji, and a Granny Smith all made it in.)

Directions

Preheat oven to 350°F. Butter a 9-by-13-inch pan. Mix the streusel ingredients in a bowl until big, crumbly bits form. Set aside.

For the cake, in a large mixing bowl, beat the eggs, butter, and oil until foamy.

Next add the flour, brown sugar, vanilla, salt, cinnamon, and baking soda. Mix until it just comes together.

Fold the diced apples into the batter. Top with the streusel topping and bake in the prepared pan 30 to 35 minutes.

Serve and enjoy.

PREP TIME
10 minutes

BAKE TIME
25–28 minutes

YIELD
1 (9-by-13-inch) cake

Rich Red Velvet Sheet Cake

Ingredients

1½ cups sugar

½ cup softened butter plus 2
tablespoons for the pans

1 tablespoon vanilla extract

½–1 teaspoon kosher salt
(depending on your taste
preference)

2 eggs, room temperature

4 tablespoons red food coloring

2½ tablespoons unsweetened
cocoa powder, sifted

2 tablespoons neutral oil

¾ teaspoon baking soda

1 cup buttermilk, divided, room
temperature

2 cups all-purpose flour, divided

CREAM CHEESE ICING

1 (8-ounce) package cream
cheese

3 cups confectioners' sugar

2 tablespoons heavy cream

1 teaspoon vanilla extract

1 pinch salt

Directions

Generously butter a 9-by-13-inch cake pan. Preheat oven to 350°F.

In a mixing bowl, cream the sugar, butter, vanilla, and salt until fluffy.
Add the eggs one at a time and mix until well incorporated.

Scrape down the sides of the bowl and add the food coloring, sifted
cocoa powder, and oil, then fold to incorporate.

In a separate bowl, mix the salt and baking soda into the flour.

Pour half the buttermilk into the batter and mix gently.

Pour half the flour into the batter and gently mix. Add the remaining
buttermilk and gently mix. Finish with the second half of the flour,
mixing just until it comes together.

Pour the batter into the pan and bake 25 to 28 minutes.

Allow the cakes to rest for 10 minutes and turn them out to cool on a
parchment-lined cooling rack.

For the icing, in a large mixing bowl using a hand mixer, cream the
cream cheese and sugar until smooth, add the heavy cream, vanilla, and
salt.

Frost once cakes are completely cool to the touch. And enjoy!

PREP TIME
15 minutes

BAKE TIME
45–55 minutes

YIELD
1 standard Bundt cake

Brown Butter Chocolate Bundt Cake

Ingredients

1 cup butter

2 cups sugar

1¾ cups all-purpose flour

1 shy cup cocoa powder (shy meaning barely full)

4 eggs

½ cup plain Greek yogurt or sour cream

1 tablespoon baking powder

1 tablespoon vanilla extract

½ teaspoon kosher salt

1 cup boiling water or coffee

1 cup of your favorite chocolate chips

FUDGE GLAZE

1 cup heavy cream

½ cup butter

½ cup cocoa powder

½ cup sugar

1 pinch salt

1 teaspoon vanilla extract

Directions

Preheat oven to 350°F. Spray the inside of a Bundt pan with cooking spray or butter and flour the inside. (I use Baker's Joy spray along with flour.) Brown the butter in a saucepan over medium to medium-high heat, roughly 6 to 8 minutes. Swirl the butter often to avoid burning. It should turn a deep brown. Pour the butter in a heat-proof bowl to cool slightly.

Place the sugar, flour, cocoa powder, eggs, Greek yogurt, baking powder, vanilla, and salt into a large mixing bowl, and mix with a hand mixer or in your stand mixer.

While the mixer is mixing, stream in the browned butter (warm but not boiling), followed by the boiling water or coffee. Make sure to scrape down the sides of the bowl. Add the chocolate chips, then mix to combine.

Pour the batter evenly into the prepared Bundt pan and bake 45 to 55 minutes. Do not overbake. Mine comes out perfect at 45 to 47 minutes.

While the cake bakes, make the glaze. Melt all the ingredients except the vanilla in a saucepan over medium heat until the sugar dissolves, 5 to 6 minutes. Do not boil.

Remove from heat and add the vanilla. Pour into a bowl to cool while the cake bakes.

After the cake is baked, cool 10 minutes, then turn it out onto a large cake plate or dinner plate. Cool completely before glazing. The cake and glaze should be at room temperature before glazing. Enjoy!

PREP TIME
20 minutes

BAKE TIME
25–30 minutes

INACTIVE TIME
2–4 hours

YIELD
1 (double-layer 9-inch) cake

Boozy Pumpkin Layer Cake with Glossy Fudge Frosting

Ingredients

1 cup packed dark brown sugar

1 cup granulated sugar

½ cup salted butter, softened

3 eggs, room temperature

1½ cups (just shy of a 15-ounce can) canned pumpkin purée

1 tablespoon vanilla extract

1½ teaspoons cinnamon

½ teaspoon ground nutmeg or pumpkin pie spice

2 cups all-purpose flour

2 teaspoons baking powder

½ teaspoon baking soda

½ teaspoon kosher salt

WHISKEY SYRUP

¾ cup granulated sugar

¼ cup whiskey of choice

GLOSSY FUDGE FROSTING

1 cup butter

1 cup granulated sugar

1 cup unsweetened cocoa powder

4 ounces semisweet baking chocolate

1 pinch salt

1¼ cups heavy cream

1 teaspoon vanilla extract

Directions

Preheat oven to 350°F. Butter and flour 2 round (9-inch) cake pans.

In a mixing bowl, combine the sugars and butter, and mix until lightly creamed.

Add the eggs, and mix thoroughly.

Add the pumpkin, vanilla, and spices, then gently mix until it all comes together.

Fold in the flour, baking powder, baking soda, and salt until just combined.

Evenly divide the batter between the prepared pans. Bake 25 to 30 minutes or until the cakes are fully baked.

To prepare the whiskey syrup, in a small bowl, combine the sugar, ½ cup water, and whiskey, and stir. Allow to set at room temperature for up to 1 hour until all the sugar has dissolved.

To prepare the glossy fudge frosting, heat the butter, sugar, cocoa powder, baking chocolate, and salt in a medium saucepan over medium heat.

Cook 4 to 5 minutes, until it starts to bubble around the edges but isn't boiling.

Slowly add the cream to the mixture. Add the vanilla. The grainy texture will melt away, and you'll be left with thick, glossy chocolate sauce.

Cool completely (2 to 4 hours) before frosting the cake, or you'll get a thin glaze on the cake instead of a frosted look.

Tip:
To keep this nonalcoholic, just eliminate the whiskey syrup, and if you'd still like a syrup soak, baste the cake with a simple syrup with no whiskey. It's still yummy!

To cool the frosting quickly, place the warm frosting into a bowl, then place the bowl into a larger bowl filled with ice and water.

To assemble the double-layer cake, place one cake onto a cake plate. With a pastry brush, apply the whiskey syrup onto one cake. Let stand 3 to 4 minutes. Next, apply a thick layer of frosting to the center. Place the second cake on top and follow the same steps to apply the whiskey syrup and the frosting. The sides can remain frosted or unfrosted according to your preference. For a 4-layer cake, slice the two cakes in half horizontally, then follow the method above.

Slice and enjoy!

PREP TIME
10 minutes

BAKE TIME
35–40 minutes

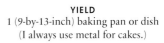

YIELD
1 (9-by-13-inch) baking pan or dish
(I always use metal for cakes.)

Chocolate Chip Pumpkin Bread

I used to own a restaurant, and I'd always tell my staff that just because I love something, doesn't mean it belongs on the menu. If it doesn't sell, it's outta here! Enter this pumpkin bread. I believe this is the most delicious pumpkin bread you will ever eat, and I first published it in my book *Meant to Share*. The recipe was once submitted to an all-star baking site, and it was either loved and applauded or despised by all who tried it, about 50/50. I'd try to show people how to make it the way I did, but honestly it was just not the perfect recipe. So, I took the advice and revamped this guy. I'm glad I did; recipes are made to be improved upon continually. Please try this one. You won't be disappointed—it is damn near perfect! Try a little cream cheese frosting if you are feeling extra!.

Ingredients

2 cups packed dark brown sugar

½ cup butter, softened

2 tablespoons neutral oil

3 eggs, room temperature

1 cup pumpkin purée

2 teaspoons vanilla extract

1 teaspoon kosher salt

½ teaspoon ground cinnamon

1¾ cups all-purpose flour

1 cup semisweet chocolate chips

1 tablespoon baking powder

½ tablespoon baking soda

½ cup full-fat buttermilk

Directions

Preheat oven to 350°. Generously butter and lightly flour your baking pan, then set aside.

Cream the sugar and butter in a mixing bowl, using a hand or stand mixer on low speed.

Add the oil and eggs one at a time, mixing on low speed after each addition.

Add the pumpkin, vanilla, salt, and cinnamon. Mix until just combined.

Add the flour, chocolate chips, baking powder, and baking soda, then mix by hand gently until flour is just incorporated.

Add the buttermilk last, and gently combine. Do not overmix.

Pour the batter into the prepared baking pan and bake 25 minutes, then check the cake with a toothpick to see if it is fully baked.

Bake an additional 5 to 10 minutes or until the cake is completely cooked but not overbaked.

Serve and enjoy!

PREP TIME
20 minutes

BAKE TIME
28–32 minutes

YIELD
1 (9-by-13-inch) cake

Bangin' Chocolate Cake with Peanut Butter Fluff Frosting

We need "wow" cake in our arsenals. We need a cake that's like, okay, yum! A cake worthy of a birthday or a barbecue, simple yet INCREDIBLE, a crowd-pleaser. If you like peanut butter and chocolate, you need this cake! If you feel like having fun with it, don't be afraid to chop up a few peanut butter cups to sprinkle on top.

Ingredients

2 cups granulated sugar

1¾ cups all-purpose flour

1 cup melted butter

1 cup buttermilk

½ cup cocoa powder

4 eggs

1 tablespoon baking powder

2 teaspoons vanilla extract

½ teaspoon kosher salt

1 (3-ounce) dark chocolate
   baking bar, melted

½ cup boiling hot water or coffee

PEANUT BUTTER FLUFF FROSTING

1 (8-ounce) package cream
   cheese, softened

1 cup of your favorite peanut butter

4 tablespoons butter, softened

3–4 cups confectioners' sugar

1 teaspoon vanilla extract

1 pinch salt

½ cup roasted salted peanuts, for
   topping

Directions

Preheat oven to 350°F. Butter, flour, and then line a 9-by-13-inch baking pan with parchment paper.

In a large mixing bowl add the sugar, flour, butter, buttermilk, cocoa powder, eggs, baking powder, vanilla, and salt. Gently mix.

Once it comes together, add the melted chocolate and water or coffee, then mix until smooth, making sure to scrape down the sides of the bowl.

Pour the batter into the prepared pan.

Bake roughly 28 to 32 minutes, being careful not to overbake.

For the frosting, cream the cream cheese, peanut butter, and softened butter together in a mixing bowl just until it turns smooth.

Scrape down the sides of the bowl, then add the confectioners' sugar, vanilla, and salt. Mix well.

Once the cake is cool, dollop the peanut butter fluff onto the cake and sprinkle the peanuts on top.

Serve and enjoy!

Tip:
Any dark chocolate
baking bar works.
I used Cadbury.

PREP TIME
15 minutes

BAKE TIME
45–55 minutes

YIELD
1 (9-by-13-inch) sheet pan

Buttermilk Yellow Sheet Cake with Glossy Fudge Frosting

I'm a sucker for a yellow cake. I have one in my book *Generations*, but I've grown since writing that recipe. I can admit when a recipe needs improvement. Over the years, many a faithful baker has written me wondering why their cakes have turned out like delicious cookie bars, not quite the yellow cake promised.

I've made and remade that recipe since, and honestly I think it's a combination of over mixing *and* the weather. So, as one does, you rework, and you come up with a simple one-bowl sheet cake that's sure to rise!

I took my buttermilk pound cake recipe from *My Heart's Table* and reworked it to be a lighter sheet cake. Combine that with the fudgy, glossy frosting found in my great granny Thora's recipe box, and you've got a cake that should have *been* from the beginning, a cake that won't turn out like a delicious cookie bar when you want a slice of cake.

Ingredients

CAKE

1 cup neutral oil like canola

1 cup buttermilk

5 eggs

2 teaspoons vanilla extract

1½ cups sugar

2¼ cups flour

2 tablespoons baking powder

1 vanilla bean, scraped (optional)

Pinch of salt

Directions

Preheat the oven to 350°. For the cake, combine all the wet cake ingredients and mix until they just come together.

Add the sugar, then mix.

Add the remaining dry ingredients and mix. Do not overmix; you want a tender crumb. Make sure you really get the flour evenly distributed within the wet ingredients.

Line a metal baking pan with parchment paper or butter, then flour it. Pour the cake batter over the top.

Bake 40 to 50 minutes. The top will turn a deep golden brown. Cool completely before frosting.

To make the frosting, heat the butter, sugar, cocoa powder, chocolate, and salt in a medium-sized saucepan over medium heat.

Cook 4 to 5 minutes until it starts to bubble around the edges but isn't boiling.

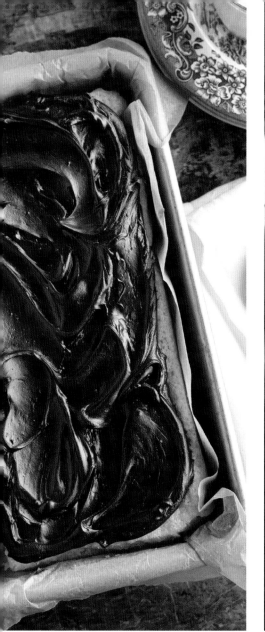

Tip:
No buttermilk? No problem. Use 1 cup of milk and 1 tablespoon white vinegar to substitute. Mix the vinegar into the milk, give it a stir, and pour into the batter. The milk will curdle, but that's just fine.

FROSTING

1 cup butter

1 cup sugar

1 cup unsweetened cocoa powder

4 ounces semisweet bakers' chocolate

Pinch of salt

1¼ cups heavy cream

1 teaspoon vanilla

Slowly add the cream to the chocolate. The grainy texture will melt away, and you'll be left with thick, glossy chocolate sauce. Stir in the vanilla.

Cool completely (2 to 4 hours) before frosting the cake or you'll get a thin glaze on the cake instead of a frosted look.

To cool the frosting quickly, place the warm frosting in a bowl, then place the bowl in a larger bowl of ice. Whisk until chilled.

Frost the chilled cake and enjoy!

Closing Thoughts

There is a lot of failing that goes into making a good cake. In fact, baking a cake is a lot like living: lots of failing and lots of getting back up again only to fail once more. Tough crumbs! When Mike left his steady job five years ago to chase this dream we have for showing people love through food, we both knew it wasn't going to be easy, but we had each other, big dreams, and the Lord nudging us onward into the unknown.

We've had big, beautiful breaks along with lots of tough-crumbs times these last several years. Sometimes things don't go as planned, and life can feel a bit unraveled. I used to question if this was the right path. I'd think, Gosh, Danielle, it'd be so much easier to work for someone else. Maybe this will be the last year you run this business. Those feelings used to happen often. But sure enough, the storm would settle, and I'd look back and know that running Rustic Joyful Food was and is just where I'm supposed to be. I think we've all baked a bum batch of cookies, but that doesn't mean we stop baking cookies altogether.

I used to be a terrible baker. I was impatient and hurried, and I wanted everything to turn out perfectly. My cakes and cookies wouldn't deliver, and I'd declare to myself, Well, I'm just not a good baker. Guess what? Even the best bakers have bad bakes some days. Our lives are this beautifully woven journey filled with ups, downs, good days, and bad days. All our endeavors are the same way. I am glad I never gave up on Rustic

Joyful Food. I'm glad the Lord showed me that some days just one foot in front of the other is exactly what I'm supposed to be doing.

On particularly tough days this past summer, my sweet friend Angie would show up out of the blue and drop a few dozen eggs off for me. She has beautiful chickens that produce the most scrumptious eggs you've ever tasted. I've never asked her for these treasures, and she has never charged me a penny. She just shows up and porch-drops dozens at a time. And my family loves an egg, in all its forms.

Rustic Joyful Food has been expanding and investing as much as possible. This last year, as soon as money came in, it went right out into our ventures and growth. Money was tight, and I thought again, often, Gosh, Danielle, maybe this isn't for you. Maybe growth and investing and opening new companies isn't for you. Then eggs would show up on my doorstep by the dozen, courtesy of my darling friend, eggs that were pastel, speckled, and beautifully rich in color. Inexplicably, it felt like a little nudge I needed: I was right where I was supposed to be, completely provided for.

These paths we choose may be difficult, but that doesn't mean we are not called to journey down them. Blazing trails is hard but rewarding. These little eggs must be cracked open to be enjoyed. Busted shells and tough crumbs also nourish. That's life. We get up again and keep going. We don't stop because it's rough. I hope you are reminded with each failure you experience, in baking or in life, that your endeavor is worthwhile! Even if it doesn't sometimes feel like it, you can be good at motherhood and relationships and baking, all at once. Don't overmix, don't overthink, just keep on going. Fix what needs fixing and look for the God winks, those little signs, pats on the back, and moments of true love that come through speckled eggs dropped on the porch and tough cookies still enjoyed by the tiniest people you love.

Break all of the eggs, enjoy them, and breathe in this joyful gift of a life.

Index

Note: Page numbers in italic refer to illustrations.

C

About the Author

DANIELLE KARTES

Danielle Kartes is an author, recipe maven, and speaker living near Seattle, Washington, with her husband, Michael, a photographer; and their two sweet boys. Together, the Karteses run their boutique food, lifestyle, and commercial photography business, Rustic Joyful Food. Rustic Joyful Food promotes loving your life right where you are, no matter where you are, and creating beautiful, delicious food that's fuss-free with whatever you have available to you. Their newest venture is the creation of Florescence Grapefruit & Pomelo Vodka. Danielle is driven by her love for Jesus, her family, and happy accidents in the kitchen. She has written and published four cookbooks, seven children's books, and one devotional memoir. Danielle appears often on national television and is the regular culinary contributor to *The Kelly Clarkson Show*.